Yorkshire Dales Walks with Children

Stephen Rickerby

Published by Sigma Leisure – an imprint of
Sigma Press, 5 Alton Road, Wilmslow, Cheshire SK9 5DY, England.

British Library Cataloguing in Publication Data
A CIP record for this book is available from the British Library.

ISBN: 978-1-85058-847-4 (13-digit); 1-85058-847-3 (10-digit)

Typesetting and Design by: Sigma Press, Wilmslow, Cheshire.

Cover photographs, clockwise from top left: Cottage garden, late summer *(Graham Beech)*; Locomotive 68005 departing from Bolton Abbey *(by kind permission of Yorkshire Dales Railway Museum Trust)*; Ribblehead viaduct *(Graham Beech)*; Above Gordale Scar *(Country Matters Picture Library; Copyright, Terry Marsh)*; Aysgarth Falls *(Graham Beech)*; Dentdale from Dent village *(Graham Beech)*

Maps: Jeremy Semmens

Printed by: Bell & Bain Ltd, Glasgow

Disclaimer: the information in this book is given in good faith and is believed to be correct at the time of publication. No responsibility is accepted by either the author or publisher for errors or omissions, or for any loss or injury howsoever caused. Only you can judge your own fitness, competence and experience. Do not rely solely on sketch maps for navigation; we strongly recommend the use of appropriate Ordnance Survey (or equivalent) maps.

Preface

The Yorkshire Dales presents a varied and fascinating landscape in which to walk with children. The walks chosen for this book attempt to reflect that variety. Scenery ranges from classic dales limestone as at Malham (Walk 19) to quiet and gentle lower valley topography as at Bolton Abbey (Walk 20) in lower Wharfedale; from high moorland wilderness at Ribblehead (Walk 8) to the cultured, human-created grounds of magnificent Fountains Abbey (Walk 10).

Particular sites such as waterfalls like Aysgarth Falls (Walk 6) and Hardraw Force (Walk 5) in Wensleydale, the awesome Ribblehead Viaduct heritage monument (Walk 8) and the historic ruins of Bolton and Fountains Abbeys (Walks 20 and 10 respectively) are well featured. Castles at Middleham and Castle Bolton (Walks 7 and 3) and the steam railway at Embsay (Walk 21) are further child-friendly attractions.

Walking with children necessitates a degree of forward planning and the walks are introduced with information about vital matters like where the toilets are, where refreshments may be found, how pushchairable a route is likely to be (usually which sections of it may be reasonably attempted) and what the terrain is basically like. This is intended to assist your planning, but the onus must remain on you to consider the aptitude of your individual children for a particular walk, at a particular season and in particular weather conditions.

All the walks have been chosen because they are potentially interesting experiences for children and are not too demanding. They are meant for children to walk with adult guidance – paths can be slippery and roads have traffic even in the hills. The majority include sections of open country walking which require strong and sensible footwear for the pedestrian, if not the back-packed child. Sensible protection against the weather – rain or shine – is also a factor on a walk which may take a small child a mile or more from the nearest road or shop.

It is a regrettable reality that in an area such as this nappy changing facilities are not especially widespread. Where they are – usually at the National Park Centres, but also most impressively at Fountains Abbey, the fact is recorded in the appropriate walk details.

Maps are suggested for each walk. The Ordnance Survey Leisure Maps are the best and are widely available in bookshops, including those at the National Park Centres. The three such sheets which cover the Yorkshire Dales map all the footpaths used in this book save for Walk 14, Wath in Nidderdale, and Walk 10, Fountains Abbey. Map details for these are given individually.

The checklists of things for children to look out for along the walk are all based on what we have actually seen. Some sights are inevitably seasonal and some you may just miss. So set a target of seeing 6 or 7, rather than all 10, to avoid disappointment.

If the "smiley face" text passages are read out as a script to children (or even if they just read it themselves) it may make for very stilted conversation. They are intended as prompts to stimulate discussion along the way. Background information in smaller "script" text should provide some back-up for fielding penetrating questions.

General thoughts such as allowing older or more confident children to find the route ahead or identify features such as tree types may help involve them better than sticking to the prepared passages here. A colleague of mine advises that she interests her children in walking by calling it exploring and avoiding the w-word altogether. Painting the experience as adventure and investigation may well be a sound approach to take with many children.

The starting and finishing points are intended to offer somewhere to go before, or more likely after, the walk. In a popular location such as Grassington (Walk 17) there will be lots of shops and refreshments, sight-seeing and craft workshop or museum visiting. Smaller places like Wath in Nidderdale may just offer a pub or café or picnic spot. However, suggestions are also made for some places nearby to drive on to – always in a matter of minutes.

Acknowledgments

I would like to express my thanks to my wife Debbie and my daughter Katie for accompanying me and helping me with these walks, to Peter and Pauline Lenney for their Hawes route and to Val Hart for her "exploring, not walking" tip.

Typestyle Conventions

To make the book easy to use, you'll find different styles of text:

"Bold" text, just like this, to give directions for the adults.

☺ Plain text with a smiley face to pick out interesting features of the walk for children (& grown ups too!) We use the same style for quiz questions.

Smaller, script-style, text like this for background information.

Enjoy your walks with children in the Yorkshire Dales. At the risk of sounding like a television safety commercial, you and your children will do so all the more if you plan and prepare in advance of setting out.

Stephen Rickerby

Contents

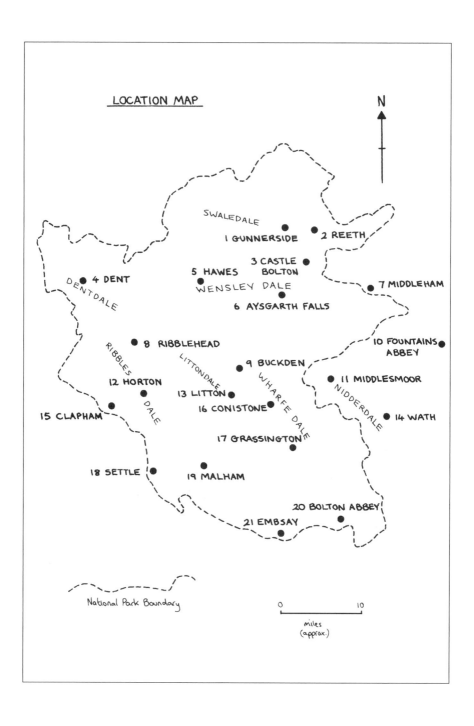

LOCATION MAP

N

SWALEDALE

1 GUNNERSIDE   2 REETH

3 CASTLE
BOLTON

5 HAWES
WENSLEY DALE   7 MIDDLEHAM

D E N T D A L E   4 DENT

6 AYSGARTH FALLS

8 RIBBLEHEAD   10 FOUNTAINS
                                   ABBEY

RIBBLES
           LITTONDALE
                       9 BUCKDEN

12 HORTON   11 MIDDLESMOOR

DALE   13 LITTON   WHARFE DALE   NIDDERDALE

15 CLAPHAM   16 CONISTONE   14 WATH

                    17 GRASSINGTON

18 SETTLE   19 MALHAM

                              20 BOLTON ABBEY

                    21 EMBSAY

National Park Boundary

0   10

miles
(approx.)

1. Gunnerside

This is a fairly easy walk in Swaledale, along the riverbank and on clear paths across pastures, returning to the pretty village of Gunnerside via a quiet lane with panoramic views over the dale.

It's a walk that's suitable for any season and is particularly rewarding in autumn when leaves are brown and wild berries are ripening.

Starting point: The Post Office in Gunnerside (SD 951982)

Distance: Route A, 3 miles; Route B, 1¼ miles

Terrain: Mostly on the level along riverside and cross-pasture grassy paths, with just one or two short steeper sections, or on metalled lanes with a steepish climb up from Ivelet to Dyke Heads.

Map: OL30 Yorkshire Dales: Northern and Central Areas.

Public Toilets: In Gunnerside village, signposted down the lane in front of the Kings Head pub, opposite the Post Office.

Refreshments: In Gunnerside, the Kings Head serves bar meals and has tables outside, the Ghyllfoot tea room and restaurant is licensed and the Post Office (Bridge Stores) sells hot bacon and other rolls, pork pies and ice cream.

Pushchairs: The section from Ivelet Bridge to Gunnerside via Dyke Heads is fine, although the climb up to Dyke Heads may be a bit of an effort. It is not possible to pushchair between Gunnerside Bridge and Ivelet on the riverside section or over the fields.

☺ You should pass most of these things on your walk. See how many you can spot.

☐ a beech tree

☐ a stone bridge

☐ a pheasant

☐ an old red telephone box

☐ a seat with some-one's name on it

☐ a sign to Muker

☐ a hay bale

☐ a house called Jubilee

☐ a dry stone wall

☐ an old bath with a new use

☐ an ash tree

☐ a cattle grid

Start the walk at Gunnerside Post Office. Stand opposite the shop, facing it. Head left down the lane towards Gunnerside Bridge.

On reaching Gunnerside Bridge do not cross it. Instead look for the narrow passage on the right-hand side and descend a few stone steps, through a wooden gate, to the waymarked riverside path. Walk along the path, away from the bridge, towards a wooden stile.

☺ The bridge here has buttresses to make it stronger so it will not easily collapse if there is a flood. The large boulders on the river bed are moved by the river when it is in flood.

Q: What type of tree is the first one on this path?

A: Sycamore

The path between Gunnerside and Ivelet is the Corpse Way. Until the late sixteenth century the only church was at Grinton which is the other side of Reeth and relatives of deceased people from the upper dale would have to carry their bodies in baskets along this path to have them buried. Traditional resting places developed where the pall bearers would put down their load.

Cross the wooden stile and walk on under the trees. on your right is a dry stone wall.

☺ Look out for beech and ash trees along here. Can you see the school in the village and the two-storey chapel we saw when we started?

Pass over a short section of path where tree roots are exposed.

☺ The large boulders in the river bank have been put here by people to strengthen it so the river does not erode it away. Notice that this is done on the outside bank of the river bend where the current is stronger.

☺ A river bend is called a meander.

Cross the second stile to walk along the grassy path beyond.

☺ Children may want to run ahead at this point. A good point to tell them where to wait is where the path goes through a gap in the dry stone wall. There are wildflowers along here to look for.

Bear right where the path passes through a gap in the dry stone wall by an ash tree. head left, dry stone wall on your left.

☺ On the slope ahead are terracettes. They look like lots of steps in the grassy bank, but are caused by the soil creeping down the steep gradient.

At the point where a dry stone wall comes down from the right to cross your path, pass through the gap in the wall and continue to walk ahead.

☺ Look at the river bank here. You can see where the river has cut underneath the bank. This is on the outer bank again.

Look for a waymark post set to the right of the path on a low mound. Turn right here, in the direction indicated Gunnerside, almost back on yourselves, and go up to the stile at the top of the rise.

☺ Look at the sign at the top.

Q: Which way should we go to reach Ivelet?

A: Left.

Cross the stile. Turn left and walk along with the fence on your left.

Route B: Head right instead and follow the path over the fields to Gunnerside village, about half a mile (800 metres).

Route A:

☺ We have to stay in single file along here.

Q: Why do you think that is?
A: So as not to trample on the grass that the animals need to eat.

☺ Look down to the fields on the other side. There is an unusually curved sheep enclosure. You can see the dry stone wall sweeping around it.

Pass through the small wooden gate in the dry stone wall ahead, ignoring metal gates to the left and right. Walk ahead.

There is a steep drop to the left of the path beyond the gate.

Negotiate the stone stile you reach next to a sign explaining the need for single file walking.

☺ The sign here says this is winter feed for stock. That means it is for the sheep to eat in the winter. We have to take care not to spoil it by trampling the pasture.

Follow the clear grass path ahead and pass through the next stone stile which is beside a green metal gate.

☺ The building here is called a Dales barn. Animals can be sheltered here and the farmer can use it to store feed such as hay for the sheep to eat if there is snow.

Keep following this pattern of crossing pastures and passing through stone stiles until you reach a gap in a dry stone wall immediately to the right on the gable end of a Dales barn. Pass through and descend the path to the right with the wood-railed fence on your left.

Cross the foot bridge at the bottom of the hollow.

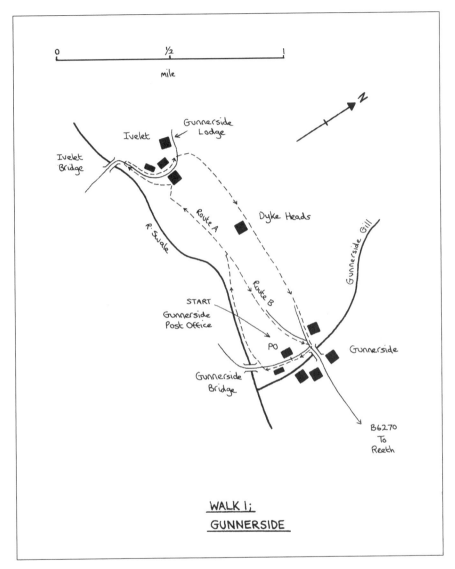

WALK 1;
GUNNERSIDE

☺ Look at the rock here. It is in layers called beds. Look out for foxgloves, if there are any in bloom, as we go up the other side.

Climb up the other side towards the buildings and emerge by salt pie cottage.

Q: What is Salt Pie Cottage used for?
A: The Estate Office.

Walk straight ahead along the initially gravelly track, and pass Ivelet farmhouse on your right. Proceed as far as the old-style telephone box at the end. Turn left down the lane in the direction of Muker.

Short-cut: turn right instead and walk up the minor road in the direction signed Gunnerside to save the walk down to Ivelet Bridge and back (saves half a mile and about 15 minutes).

Walk down the hill and follow the metalled lane as it swings right.

☺ At the bottom there are some place where we can go up to the water's edge and skip spinning stones over the water. Look out for birds on the river.

Dippers are water birds to be found on this reach of the Swale. They are brown birds with a white chest and dip underwater for their food.

At Ivelet Bridge walk to the high point of this single span.

Look at the view up and down the river.

Q: Which river is this?
A: The Swale

Turn back.

As you leave the bridge look on the ground for a rectangular stone which was a traditional resting place along the Corpse Way.

Retrace your steps to Ivelet itself.

There are a number of brambles to be found on your left and in season there will be blackberries to pick.

☺ Look out for blackberry bushes along here.

Walk up the minor road in the direction signed Gunnerside, towards the cattle grid. Keep following the road uphill.

At the hairpin bend, stop to admire the view.

☺ From here we can see a long away along Swaledale.

At Gunnerside Lodge take the right fork down to the cattle grid. Over this, climb again to Jingle Pot Lodge.

☺ The house on the right has an unusual name. Look out for it and an old bath used as a drinking trough for animals.

Continue along the quiet lane.

From the lane there are panoramic views of Swaledale. Looking down from your vantage point you can see low hummocky ridges stretched out along the sides of the flat valley floor. These are suggestive of material deposited by a glacier during the Ice Age.

☺ The bumps at the bottom of the valley sides are made of moraine – material dumped there by a glacier during the Ice Age. The last Ice Age was around 18 000 years ago.

By the time you reach Dyke Heads you can see Gunnerside Bridge where you may have parked and the children may well be able to identify your car.

The lane will take you down into Gunnerside village. Head into the centre, towards the Kings Head.

Gunnerside, Swaledale *(Graham Beech)*

☺ All the houses in Gunnerside village have names. Look for one with no vowels in its name.

It is called Whyllsyn.

The Village Stores and Post Office doubles as a craft and painting gallery and sells ice creams, sandwiches and snacks. The public toilets are over the bridge and down the alleyway to the right in front of the Kings Head.

The chapel is down the lane towards Gunnerside Bridge.

Q: When was the chapel built?
A: 1866

Other Places of Interest in the Area

Reeth

Reeth (Walk 2) is a stone-built village surrounding a large open green. It has plenty of cafés, pubs serving food and ice cream shops and there are a variety of craft workshops you could visit, as well as the Swaledale Folk Museum. Reeth Show is in late autumn; market day is Friday.

The Waterfalls at Keld

Travelling up-valley, Keld is the last village in Swaledale. Cartrake Force is close to the village and Kisdon Force is about half a mile downstream on the same southern bank of the Swale. The path is steep however and not suitable for very young children.

Richmond Castle

Richmond is the market town of Swaledale. Its ruined Norman Castle is approached from the cobbled market square. The keep and two towers remain to stimulate a child's imagination. Richmond Castle is open daily from April to October (Tel: 01748 822493).

2. Reeth

Reeth is a large Dales village centred on a green, around which imposing stone buildings are arranged. There is a wealth of cafés and pubs offering bar food. A small market is held on Fridays. In Reeth, you can visit the Swaledale Folk Museum and there is a variety of craft workshops including a cabinet-maker, a guitar-maker and a maker of model animals.

Starting point: Town green, Reeth (SE 038992)

Distance: 3 miles

Terrain: Mostly across pastureland with sections of surfaced lane

Map: OL30 Yorkshire Dales: Northern and Central Areas.

Public Toilets: Reeth

Refreshments: Reeth and Grinton

Pushchairs: The cross-pasture upper section is not suitable for pushchairs though the lane parts of the route would be.

☺ You should pass most of these things on your walk. See how many you can spot.

- ☐ an old-fashioned lamp-post
- ☐ an upside-down pub sign
- ☐ a water fountain
- ☐ a chapel clock
- ☐ a black-faced sheep
- ☐ limestone outcrops
- ☐ a dry stone wall
- ☐ lambs
- ☐ nests

☐ black cattle

☐ a church tower

☐ a sign to a priory

From the town green, walk down the hill, alongside the road, to cross Reeth Bridge.

Stop on Reeth Bridge.

☺ The river here is Arkle Beck which is a tributary of the River Swale. Reeth is in Swaledale.

Q: Which way is Arkle Beck flowing?

A: Away from Reeth (south)

On the other side of the bridge turn right alongside the road and round the bend. Follow the public footpath to your left through a narrow stone stile and then immediately bear right towards a red metal gate.

Pass through the adjacent small wooden gate into the pasture to

Reeth village *(Norman Buckley)*

follow the path ahead as it bears left to another gate in the corner. Pass through this too and follow the path up to a further gate.

☺ From here we can see a lot of Swaledale and looking back we can see up the valley to Reeth where we started.

Continue onwards until you reach the farm buildings at High Fremington. Pass through the gate and follow the rough track onto the surfaced one. Continue uphill behind the farmhouse.

Q: What is the name of the restored cottage just ahead on the left?

A: The Brambles

☺ Brambles is another name for blackberry bushes. It is an old word which has been handed down from the Vikings who settled much of the Dales well over a thousand years ago.

Keep on the track as it rises and curves left to bring you to a parting of the ways. Turn left and then sharp right onto the waymarked footpath. Follow this across pasture until you reach the next gate. Pass through and cross a stony lane.

Continue straight ahead.

☺ The farmhouse on the right here is Sorrel Sykes. Keep looking down to the right and soon you should see a church by a small village – this is Grinton which we will pass through later on the walk.

Pass through the next two gates and carry straight on and through a third, small, wood gate. Here the path seems to curve right, but you should follow the dry stone wall on your left and through a gap. Continue and pass through the stile you reach to follow the dry stone wall on your right until it reaches a right angle. Now leave the wall and walk straight ahead towards the minor road which you access by means of a small wooden gate slightly to the left.

Q: What does the waymark post say?

A: Fremington

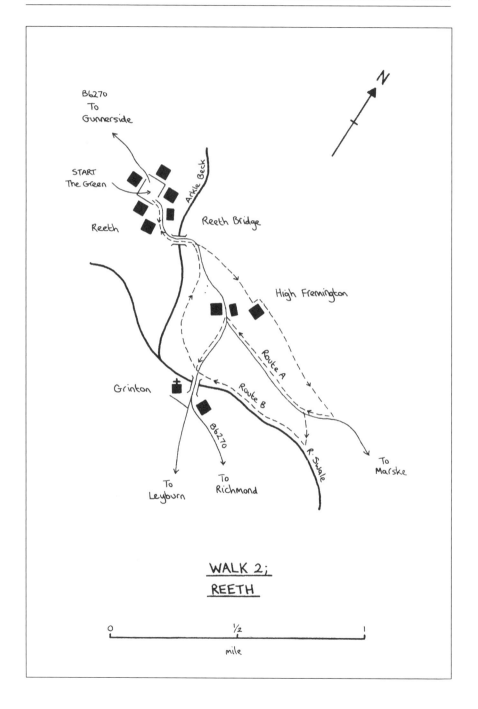

B6270
To
Gunnerside

START
The Green

Reeth

Arkle Beck

Reeth Bridge

High Fremington

Route A

Route B

Grinton

B6270

R. Swale

To
Leyburn

To
Richmond

To
Marske

N

WALK 2;
REETH

0   ½   1

mile

☺ Fremington is where we have been. The farm we walked through is called High Fremington.

Turn right and walk down the road.

The Swale can be seen to your left.

☺ The river down there is the Swale. The river we crossed at Reeth was Arkle Beck. If you remember that is a tributary of the Swale – a small river that joins this main one.

Q: Which way do you think the Swale is flowing?
A: It is moving from right to left (eastwards) as we look at it.

At the junction choose your route.

Route A: Carry on along the lane ahead to the next junction.

Escape route: Bear right at the junction and follow the road back to Reeth.

Turn left at the junction and you come to Grinton Bridge.

Both routes come together again here.

Route B: Turn left in the direction of Marrick Priory. Look for the footpath on your right and follow this along the Swale to Grinton Bridge.

Cross the bridge to have a look at Grinton and perhaps visit the inn. The church was mostly built between the 13th and 15th centuries but is partly Norman. Until the sixteenth century it was the only church in Swaledale and people from the upper dale would carry deceased people here for burial along what was known as the Corpse Way.

Part of the Corpse Way is followed in Walk 1 (Gunnerside).

Return over the bridge, recrossing the river, and turn left through a narrow gap in the stone parapet and descend the steps. The gap is waymarked by a sign on the opposite side of the road.

Follow the path ahead as it bears right towards some wooden gates.

☺ Looking at the Dalesides here you can see how narrow the fields are. One reason for this is to divide the land down the slope to make sure that each farmer has a share of lower, more sheltered, better quality pasture as well as upland grazing.

Pass through the kissing gate and continue until you pass between a wooden farm building and the river.

☺ If you look left through the trees you should be able to see the green in the middle of Reeth where we started.

Pass through a wooden gate to walk along the bank of Arkle Beck to the road. Turn left and walk over Reeth Bridge and back up to hill to the green.

Other Places of Interest in the Area

Richmond

The streets of Richmond teem outwards from its cobbled central square and are fascinating to explore. Beside the castle and shops, attractions include the Green Howards Regimental Museum (Tel: 01748 826561) and the Georgian Theatre Museum (Tel: 01748 825252). Both are open on most days from April to October. The walk down to the river and its falls is another fine day option.

Arkengarthdale

Arkengarthdale is a tributary dale of Swaledale, joining the latter at Reeth. The drive up to Arkengarthdale onto the moors will bring you, 10 miles or so later, to Britain's highest inn at Tan Hill (1732 ft above sea level). The Tan Hill Inn serves bar snacks and meals. Tel: 01833 628246.

Bolton Castle

Bolton Castle is situated in the village of Castle Bolton (Walk 3), about 5 miles west of Leyburn. The castle is square and imposing and offers great views of Wensleydale from the top of its walls. Dating from the 14th century, it houses tapestries and armour and includes Mary Queen of Scots bed-chamber (she was imprisoned here for 6 months). The castle is open from March to early November (Website: www.boltoncastle.co.uk; Tel: 01969 623981).

3. Castle Bolton

The castle is open to visitors who can see Mary Queen of Scots' bedchamber and a horse-driven mill among other attractions. There are refreshments inside. The village of Redmire is conveniently at the turning-point of this walk. There are pubs serving bar food and a shop in Redmire which, though outside the National Park, is still an attractive village.

Starting point: Castle Bolton car park (SE 034918)

Distance: 2½ miles

Terrain: After beginning along the village street, the walk crosses fields to and from Redmire Village. There are further sections of lanes too. The final part is uphill though not very steeply so.

Map: OL30 Yorkshire Dales: Northern and Central Areas

Public Toilets: Castle Bolton

Refreshments: Redmire

Pushchairs: The two villages themselves are the limit of pushchairability.

☺ You should pass most of these things on your walk. See how many you can spot:

☐ St Oswald's church

☐ a sign to Reeth

☐ train buffers

☐ a horse

☐ catkins

☐ a railway bridge

☐ a bell

☐ a sundial

☐ a henhouse

☐ a silo

☐ a drinking trough

☐ a plaque for George Jackson

Turn left out of the car park entrance and walk the length of the street of Castle Bolton village.

Bolton Castle from Walk 6 *(Graham Beech)*

☺ This is Bolton Castle **(INDICATE RIGHT)**. It is over 500 years old and was built for Sir Richard Scrope – a local knight who rose to become Chancellor of the Exchequer in London.

☺ The towers are 100 feet (just over 30 metres) high. Mary Queen of Scots was imprisoned here for 6 months in 1568.

☺ The village is called Castle Bolton after the castle. Look out for a waymark post to tell us how far it is to Redmire which is where we turn round.

It is 1.5 miles.

Where the road turns left at the end, you should take the right, unmade, fork and then turn right following the signposted public footpath to Redmire.

Pass a farm building on your left and walk through the gateway. Watch the dry stone wall on your left carefully for a narrow stone stile.

If you walk as far as a red gate, you have gone too far.

Beyond the stile, head diagonally across the pasture, bearing slightly right. Pass through the small gate set in the dry stone wall and continue to the field corner to cross a small footbridge.

Reaching the disused railway line, head left keeping the fence between yourself and the old railway to your right.

Cross the next footbridge.

☺ Now we are where the modern single track railway ends.

Q: How can we tell?

A: We can see the buffers.

Emerge at a minor road and turn right along it into Redmire.

☺ As we go down here see if you can tell which house used to be the old school.

It is Addlebrough Cottage.

Walk on to the Bolton Arms and explore the village. There is also the Kings Arms and the post office shop.

☺ See if you can find an old, gnarled tree which has to be supported on wooden posts.

After exploring Redmire, walk back to the Bolton Arms and, beyond, take the public footpath indicated to your left. Cross the stile you reach and from the waymarker corner head for the stile in the dry stone wall opposite. Pass through and turn left along the edge of the pasture.

Go through the next stone stile and walk alongside the wall which separates the field from the stream. Approach the farm at Northgate Bridge. Pass over the stile to the road and turn right.

Look out for the Yorkshire Dales National Park sign.

☺ We are now coming back into the Yorkshire Dales National Park – Redmire is just outside it. National Parks are areas of countryside which are specially protected for us to enjoy and to keep wild areas safe for the future. They are not owned by the government but by the farmers and landowners of the area. However, there are restrictions on what new building can take place, for example, to keep the area attractive.

Turn right at the junction, following alongside the road.

☺ We can see Bolton Castle again now – that's where we are aiming.

Walk round the left bend.

☺ Look carefully along the hedge here for the waymarked footpath we want – to Castle Bolton.

Turn right onto the path and follow it across the pasture to a stile directly opposite. Over this you continue to walk and pass through three wooden gates between fields before bearing left to a dry stone

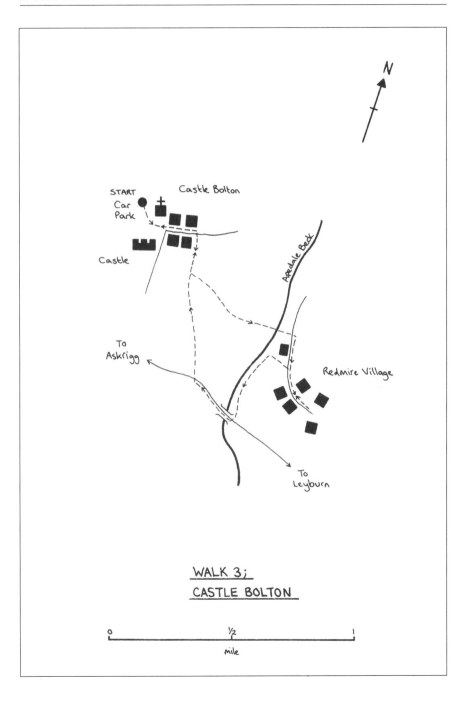

N

START
Car
Park

Castle Bolton

Castle

Apedale Beck

To
Askrigg

Redmire Village

To
Leyburn

WALK 3;
CASTLE BOLTON

0   ½   1
mile

wall. Go through the small gate here and turn sharply right to walk up to a stile.

☺ This is the cutting used by the old railway which used to go right up Wensleydale, but now stops at Redmire. The Wensleydale Railway Association are campaigning to open the line to Redmire to passenger trains and then to rebuild it from Redmire west to Garsdale where it would join the Settle-Carlisle line.

This dismantled railway is also crossed by the Aysgarth Falls walk (6). If you have already done that you could point out that it is only 2 miles west (left) of here. Similarly the Ribblehead walk (8) crosses the Settle-Carlisle line only a few miles south of Garsdale – a restored railway would link all these places together.

Cross the cutting and walk along the right-hand side of the gully to cross the waymarked stile further up and join a farm track. Walk straight ahead back to Castle Bolton village, turning left along the street to the castle itself and the car park to its right.

Other Places of Interest in the Area

Leyburn

The thriving market town of Leyburn is the gateway to Wensleydale. The large market square is fringed by numerous shops, cafés and pubs serving meals. Market day is Friday. On the edge of town (A684 towards Bedale) is an unusual teapot factory open to visitors (Tel: 01937 588235).

White Rose Candle Workshop, Wensley

The candle workshop is housed in Wensley Mill about 2 miles west of Leyburn. You can watch the candles being made and can buy them too – as presents perhaps. It is open from June to November as well as at Easter and Bank-holidays, but it is closed Wednesdays and Saturdays (Tel: 01969 623544).

Reeth

See Walk 2.

4. Dent

Dentdale is one of only two western facing dales in the national park – the other is Garsdale to the north. It is quieter than many and very pretty – quite reminiscent of Greendale in the Postman Pat stories.

Dent itself is a huddled village with cobbled streets. The white-washed buildings make a striking change from other Dales villages.

The walk begins and ends in Dent village where there is a wide range of facilities and takes in a stroll along the banks of the river Dee and return route across pasture, offering good views up the dale.

Starting point: National Park car park, Dent (SD 704872)

Distance: Route A, 2½ miles; Route B, 2¾ miles

Terrain: Initially a riverside path and then a short steeper section up the Daleside to return to Dent across quite heavy pastureland.

Map: OL2 Yorkshire Dales: Southern and Western Areas

Public Toilets: Dent

Refreshments: Dent

Pushchairs: The walk described is not suitable for pushchairs – only the streets of Dent village, but remember these are cobbled.

☺ You should pass most of these things on your walk. See how many you can spot.

- ☐ a church clock
- ☐ cobbles
- ☐ a sycamore tree
- ☐ rose hips
- ☐ a henhouse
- ☐ a sheep with black marking
- ☐ a shepherd
- ☐ a sheep dog
- ☐ a church tower
- ☐ an ash tree
- ☐ a tent
- ☐ a waterfall

Dent village *(Graham Beech)*

The car park at Dent is surfaced with 'Grasscrete'.

😊 This car park is different.

Q: Why do you think it has been made like this?
A: To make it look more attractive. From a distance it looks like grass, but it is hardwearing so cars won't make it muddy.

From the car park entrance, turn left up the cobbled street and then turn left at the George and Dragon inn to walk down and out of the village as far as the bridge over the River Dee.

😊 The river here is called the Dee. Some of the Dales are named after their rivers (like Swaledale and Wharfedale) and others have the same name as one of their villages (like Dentdale and Wensleydale).

Begin to walk onto the bridge but do not cross it. Instead turn left through a narrow gap in the stone parapet, indicated by the waymarker.

The steps you encounter here have a guard-rail only on the right so warn children to be careful.

😊 The path here will lead us along the riverbank to Barth Bridge.

Follow the path ahead. It crosses a small footbridge and a stile.

😊 You can see Dent village over to the left. When we finish the walk we will be coming down the daleside behind the village. Dent used to be important in days gone by for knitting and more than twice as many people lived there then. People used to work in their own houses as well as in mills. When workers do that it is called a cottage industry. There are still some craft knitters there today, perhaps we could go and see one when we have finished the walk.

Cross the next stile you reach.

Escape route: Turn left here to return to Dent.

Walk on along the river bank until you emerge at the roadside.

Walk carefully alongside the road, in the same westerly direction, until you soon reach a seat on your right with a waymarked stile.

Q: Where is the waymarker pointing towards?
A: Barth Bridge, a mile.

☺ That is the way to go then.

Cross the stile and follow the riverside path.

Sometimes seagulls may be seen here.

☺ Dentdale points westwards. That means it faces in the direction of the Irish Sea. Sometimes seagulls fly inland here to feed. The wind usually blows from the west so this helps carry them up Dentdale.

Keep along side the river until it suddenly and markedly swings right and the path bears left to a stile. Cross this and walk up the steps onto Barth Bridge.

☺ As well as the main arch over the river, there are some smaller ones to the left which help lift the road over this wet meadow.

Q: How many steps are there?
A: 10

Walk up to the bridge to view up and down Dentdale, but do not cross it.

Walk away from the river, left from the top of the steps, and along the lane, but only a little way. Turn right along the waymarked footpath, over a stile with a hedgerow to your left.

☺ Look at the way this hedge has been made. What is unusual is that trees have been trained to grow their branches along the boundary to make the hedge.

This is especially clear in the case of an ash tree at the corner.

Around the corner look for a waymark stile to cross to the left of a small stone farm building. Then turn right and walk on, with the dry stone wall now on your right.

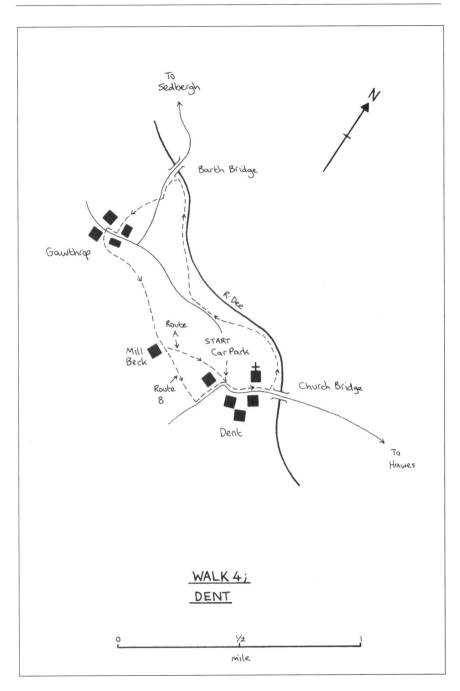

To
Sedbergh

N

Barth Bridge

Gawthrop

R. Dee

Route
A

Mill
Beck

START
Car Park

Route
B

Church Bridge

Dent

To
Hawes

WALK 4;
DENT

0   ½   1
mile

The stream on the right here can be very impressive following wet weather – quite a torrent as it cascades down its rocky course.

Keep walking up, crossing a stile, with the stream on your right.

☺ Look out for a waterfall up here.

Reaching a waymarked gate, pass through and turn left onto the metalled lane. Turn right up this into the hamlet of Gawthrop and walk up to the seat where there is a name board.

☺ Look for a sign to tell us what this place is called.

Turn left at the fork and walk up the lane which curves left ahead around the end of a row of white terraced cottages.

Q: What is the name of the last cottage?
A: Brookside

Approaching two barns, take the waymarked right fork and pass through the metal gate. Walk on to negotiate two further gates either side of a yard.

Head straight along the pasture edge, cross a stile and continue to a waymarked gate. Pass through and carry on to another gate.

☺ We can see Dent village ahead of us now. Its white-washed buildings make it look distinctive.

Beyond the gate, walk on towards the solitary tree opposite. Go through the gate and walk down the track to reach a seven bar gate. Bear slightly left to walk in front of a row of white-washed farm cottages.

Route A: **When the twin tracks of a concrete farm lane lead off to the left, follow them downhill and around a hairpin bend. Bear right, as waymarked, through a black metal gate and go straight ahead, crossing a small rail stile on the way, until you are obliged to walk left and right around a byre.**

Walk straight on to the farmyard and then turn left to emerge in Dent. Turn right to return to the car park.

Route B: Walk straight ahead at Mill Beck Farm and keep going until you reach the lane. Turn left and down into Dent, turning left again in the centre of the village to reach the car park.

Other Places of Interest in the Area

Ribblehead Viaduct

The Ribblehead Viaduct (Walk 8) is a magnificent monument to Victorian engineering. 24 arches carry the Settle-Carlisle Railway across this exposed and often cold and windy moorland expanse. You can park your car within view and easy strolling distance of the viaduct. There is a pub and often some refreshment vans.

Holme Farm, Sedbergh

This is a working farm where children can see baby animals and follow nature trails. It is open daily from March to September (Tel: 01539 620654). From Dent, drive down the dale to reach the town of Sedbergh. The farm is off the road.

Sedgwick Geological Trail, Garsdale

Garsdale parallels Dentdale to the north. Access it via Sedbergh and drive about 2 miles east along the A684 to find the trail. For further information contact the National Park Centre at Sedbergh (Tel: 01539 625231).

5. *Hawes*

Hawes is a market town in Upper Wensleydale. Its cobbled streets are frequently thronged by its many visitors. The town is the home of the Dales Countryside Museum and also, of course, of authentic Wensleydale cheese. A visitor centre is attached to the creamery.

Tuesday is market day. Livestock are still bought and sold in the town, on the main road in from Leyburn, and this adds a Dales flavour to what you might expect of the occasion.

The walk begins and ends at the National Park Centre and takes in some attractive riverside scenery along the Ure, as well as typical Dales landscape and the highest waterfall in England at Hardraw.

To reach the town centre turn right at the end of the access road to the National Park Centre which itself leads off the road in from Leyburn (the A684). Opposite the end of the access road is Hawes children's playground.

Starting point:	National Park Centre (SD 875898) adjacent to the Dales Countryside Museum.
Distance:	Route A: 3½ miles; Route B: 4½ miles
Terrain:	Initially flat on roadside and surfaced paths, the walk climbs through pasture almost to Sedbusk, before crossing many small fields and stiles to Simonstone. The return on route A is mostly over pasture, some of it on surfaced paths.
Map:	OS Explorer OL30 Yorkshire Dales: Northern and Central Areas
Public Toilets:	Hawes
Refreshments:	Hawes, Hardraw
Pushchairs:	From Hawes to the Ure and back is suitable, but the pastures and stiles limit the convenient use of pushchairs to this confined area

☺ You should pass most of these things on your walk. See how many you can spot.

☐ a cattle grid

☐ an old station

☐ black faced and white faced sheep

☐ a fire watchtower

☐ a henhouse

☐ a river meander

☐ a duck

☐ an old fashioned telephone box

☐ an aeroplane

☐ a tractor

☐ a Pennine Way sign

☐ a ropemaking factory

Hawes village *(Graham Beech)*

Begin by walking to the old station building at the back of the National Park centre's car park. Turn left up the ramp and right to cross the road bridge over the railway.

Walk down to a turning on the left where there is a cattle grid. Next to this is a stile. Cross over and walk along the flagged pathway.

☺ Looking ahead from here we can see the side of the dale. The scenery is typical of the Dales. There are dry stone walls and Dales barns scattered along them. Lower intake fields give way to open rougher pasture up the slope. There are very few trees.

Pass through the kissing gate at the end and cross the road. Walk left, along the path beyond the road.

Ahead is Haylands Bridge

☺ The bridge we are walking towards is called Haylands Bridge. We will be using it to cross the River Ure.

Cross Haylands Bridge.

☺ From the bridge we can see the river bend or meander. On the outer bank the current is stronger and the water wears away the bank to from a low, step river cliff. However, the inner bank is shallow, with a beach of pebbles and stones, because the river here is slow-flowing and leaves these deposits here.

Follow the road around to the left.

To the right of the road there is a low space in the wall which is to allow flood waters drain through.

Turn right through a gap in the dry stone wall onto a path crossing pasture.

Q: Where is this waymarked towards?
A: Sedbusk, 1¼ miles.

☺ We will be walking close to Sedbusk which is a hamlet on the daleside.

Cross a humped footbridge and follow the path up and slightly to the left. Continue beyond a stile and cross a large pasture to reach a

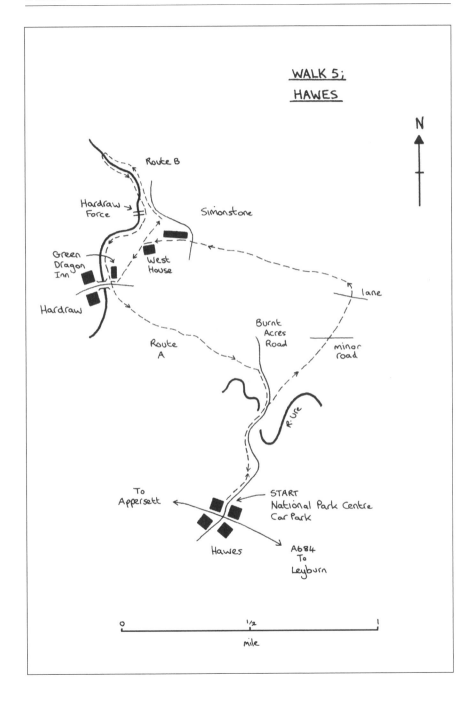

WALK 5;
HAWES

N

Route B

Hardraw
Force

Simonstone

Green
Dragon
Inn

West
House

Hardraw

lane

Burnt
Acres
Road

Route
A

minor
road

R. Ure

To
Appersett

START
National Park Centre
Car Park

Hawes

A684
To
Leyburn

0   1/2   1

mile

short flight of wooden steps up to a small wooden gate at the end of a strip of woodland.

There are views back from here over Hawes and along Wensleydale.

Cross the metalled lane and the wall opposite via the waymarked gate. Walk straight ahead up the rise in the direction of Sedbusk Lane.

It would be possible to make a detour via the hamlet of Sedbusk if you wished, by walking right at the waymarker.

At the top of the field is a dry stone wall with a stile to cross. Walk on and cross the next stile beside a Dales barn.

From here Sedbusk is visible to the right.

☺ The small settlement over there is Sedbusk. It does not have a church so it is a hamlet. After we have crossed Sedbusk Lane look along to the hamlet and you should see its old fashioned telephone box.

Q: What will that look like?

A: Red with a lot of little windows.

A further stone stile accesses Sedbusk Lane. Turn right for a few paces only before turning left onto a waymarked foot path.

Q: Where are we heading for now?

A: Simonstone

The path heads diagonally left across the enclosure to a waymark post where you turn left.

☺ Look right here and you will see the old telephone box in Sedbusk.

If you have detoured via Sedbusk you will be re-joining the main walk now.

Cross the stone stile and walk straight ahead to the gate on the other side of a narrow enclosure – the first of a series.

☺ Looking up the daleside to our right we can see where the limestone outcrops (comes to the surface). Starting with this one count how many dry stone walls we cross before we join a farm track.

Keep walking through the series of enclosure until you reach and join a farm track.

Q: How many dry stone walls have we crossed?
A: 14

Walk straight on to pass through a metal farm gate. Carry on to the metalled lane and turn left along it and then right into the driveway that leads to Simonstone Hall hotel. Before you reach the gates to its courtyard, however, turn left along the narrow path which is down a few steps.

Follow this path past the hotel grounds and down and left to West House.

There is now the option of making a detour to see the pretty wooded glade of Shaw Gill Wood. This is a mini circular walk of its own and will bring you back to this point.

Route B: **Turn hard right beyond the outbuilding on the right and follow the track up and over the ridge and down to the metalled lane. Turn left along this and begin to round a right-hand bend before taking a left turn down a walled lane which leads to a metal gate affording access to Shaw Gill Wood.**

Walk round the loop path and back across the footbridge. Re-trace your steps to West House and re-join Route A.

Route A: **Walk across the front of West House and take the waymarked footpath into a pasture. Begin the descent to Hardraw.**

On the way down the daleside there are excellent views over Wensleydale and the settlement of Hardraw is soon visible.

☺ The village down there **(INDICATE BELOW AND RIGHT)** is famous for its waterfall called Hardraw Force. This is unusual because it is supposed to be the biggest in England (a drop of 96 feet) and because you can only see it by going through the Green Dragon Inn in Hardraw.

Hardraw Force is only to be seen by paying a small charge at the Green Dragon Inn.

From the Green Dragon Inn, cross the road and walk down the path between the Shepherd's Kitchen tea room and the riverside. Bear left and follow the waymarked and initially surfaced path over the fields to Burnt Acres Road – the road to Hawes. Turn right and soon you are re-tracing your early steps back to Hawes National Park Centre.

Other Places of Interest in the Area

Aysgarth Falls

The falls at Aysgarth (Walk 6) are one of the most well-known Dales beauty spots and are therefore busy in season. Park in the National Park Centre car park where there are toilets and nappy change facilities. There are easy walks to the higher, lower and middle falls, which are well-signposted, and a nature trail. There is a café close to the higher falls which are nearest the car park. Keld waterfalls (Walk 1) are also nearby.

Askrigg

Askrigg is a small town in Wensleydale, mid-way between Leyburn and Sedbergh most famous recently as the location used for the fictional Darrowby by the makers of the "All Creatures Great and Small" television series. A pub meal can be had at the King's Arms. Askrigg is 5 miles drive east of Hawes. You may care to try the quieter back route via Hardraw and Sedbusk.

Ribblehead Viaduct

See Walk 7.

6. *Aysgarth Falls*

The falls at Aysgarth are justifiably one of the best known attractions of the Yorkshire Dales National Park. While no single fall is a record-breaker (unlike Hardraw Force, Walk 5) the fact that there are three sets of falls in such quick succession makes them none the less a dramatic sight for children to enjoy.

Starting point: National Park Centre, Aysgarth Falls (SE 013887)

Distance: Route A: 3 miles; Route B: 2½ miles; Route C: 1 mile

Terrain: Well-trodden but muddy paths take you down to the falls. Down to the Lower Falls the way is steep and can be slippy. Much of the rest of the walk is on tracks and lanes, but there are some stretches of pastureland to cross too.

Map: OS Explorer OL30 Yorkshire Dales: Northern and Central Areas.

Public Toilets and nappy change facilities: National Park Centre

Refreshments: Aysgarth Falls. There is a café at the end of the bridge by the High Falls.

Pushchairs: The way along to the Middle and Lower Falls is not viable for pushchairs unless the paths are dry. Only the area around the High Falls and Low Lane are suitable.

☺ You should pass most of these things on your walk. See how many
   you can spot:

☐ a coppiced tree

☐ a primrose

☐ a bluebell

☐ a deer

☐ a squirrel

☐ a silver birch tree

☐ catkins

☐ holly

☐ a tractor

☐ blackberry bushes

☐ a cockerel

☐ a pony

The early part of the walk is through Freeholders Wood. A trail leaflet is
available form the National Park Centre. You may wish to collect one
before you start walking.

**Walk out of the car park along the path next to the entrance drive.
Cross the road and go through the pair of gates opposite.**

Look at the information board here.

☺ This wood is called Freeholders Wood. As we walk through we will
   be able to see how the trees have been coppiced – made to grow
   many thin branches that can be used for poles.

**Follow the path as it curves left to a waymarker. Go right here to
view the middle fall and then return here.**

☺ The river which flows through Wensleydale is called the River Ure.
   The river has eroded the falls by wearing away the rock floor of its
   channel. Because the channel is made of different rock types,
   some are worn away more quickly and steps are created which
   begin the falls.

Aysgarth Falls, middle fall *(Graham Beech)*

Walk on in the direction indicated to the lower fall, passing through a kissing gate further along.

Where the way divides carry straight on in the direction of the Lower Falls viewing point. The path leads along and then dips down right to a single wooden gate giving access to the steeply descending path down to the Lower Falls, via a signposted right-hand turn on the way down.

This path can be slippy so take care.

☺ The Middle Falls we saw before used to be further downstream than they are now. The same is true of these. As water falls over the rock ledges these are undercut by the churning water and by the stones it carries so that they collapse and the whole fall retreats upstream leaving a gorge. Look for the gorge downstream of these falls.

Route C: **From the Lower Falls viewing point continue along** upstream, over the riverside stones, and follow the visitor path uphill to meet the path you used to reach the viewing point. Head left, back to the National Park Centre.

☺ Along here you can see pot-holes where the water has used stones to drill down into the rock when it is in flood. All the loose stones lying about will be picked up by the river when it is full and used to wear the rock channel away.

Route C shortcuts the walk, but if you walk along to the Higher Falls (turn left along the roadside) you will still have seen all the falls.

Route A is the full walk.

Route A: From the Lower Falls viewing point turn back on yourself to proceed downstream and then back up left to the gate. Head initially left until you see a wooden footpath guidepost on your right at the top of a rise.

☺ Go ahead and see where the waymark post guides us to.

Redmire and Castle Bolton are to the right.

Turn right and walk in their direction, passing between a wood rail fence to the left and a rocky knoll to the right. Use the fence to guide you along to a stone stile. Cross this and set off across the field ahead towards some large trees.

☺ Ahead of us now is a farm called Hollins House. That is where we are now headed – look out for a gate we need to go through.

Pass through the red metal gate and walk along the track as it rises and turns sharply left. Where tracks meet in the farm, turn right and make for the entrance gateway.

Q: What is there on this gateway to show us we are going the right way?
A: A yellow waymark sign.

Yellow paint is sometimes used to denote rights of way where there are no more formal, and often more recent, waymark posts or arrows. Yellow circles, gatepost tops and even stones on dry stone walls are common.

From the gatepost follow the drive as it curves left, avoid going

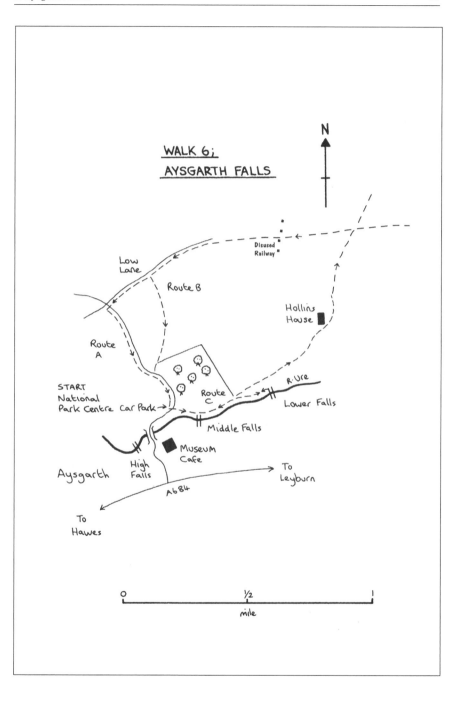

WALK 6;
AYSGARTH FALLS

N

Low
Lane

Disused
Railway

Route B

Hollins
House

Route
A

R. Ure

START
National
Park Centre Car Park→

Route
C

Lower Falls

Middle Falls

Museum
Cafe

Aysgarth

High
Falls

To
Leyburn

A684

To
Hawes

0   ½   1
                              mile

The parh crosses under the disused railway *(Graham Beech)*

through the red metal gate straight ahead. Coming to another red gate across your track, pass through it and walk on for 50m to a footpath sign pointing to the right. From here, go through a gateway with its metal gate.

Follow the well-trodden path with a fence on your right. As the fence kinks to the right, continue ahead to a gated stile. Cross this and continue towards the far corner of the field.

😊 There are great views of Castle Bolton as you cross the field. Time for a photograph!

The path continues to a stile in a wall. Do NOT cross this. Instead, turn sharp left and, with the wall on your right, head towards a wooded area. Keep straight ahead, go through a gateway and under a disused railway.

😊 There used to be a railway all the way up Wensleydale. Now it only goes as far as Redmire which is a couple of miles to the right from here. It would have made a good tourist railway if the tracks had not been taken up.

Go though two more gateways and join the tarmac farm track coming in from the left. Continue uphill for a short distance and pass through a gateway and onto a lane.

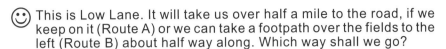 This is Low Lane. It will take us over half a mile to the road, if we keep on it (Route A) or we can take a footpath over the fields to the left (Route B) about half way along. Which way shall we go?

Route A: Continue along Low Lane to its junction with a road. To avoid traffic, turn left down the road to a stone stile on your right which is waymarked. Turn right and enter the field. Follow the path as it parallels the dry stone wall on your left to take you through a narrow gap stile ahead. Turn left onto the road and walk downhill to the National Park Centre and on to the Higher Falls.

Route B: While walking along Low Lane, pass a large building on your left, carry on for two fields and look for the waymarked path on your left. Take this and follow it over the fields and through a short stretch of woodland to the road above the National Park Centre.

Other Places of Interest in the Area

The National Park Centre, Aysgarth Falls

Located at the start of this walk, the centre is an invaluable source of local information and also includes the excellent Coppice Café. Tel: 01969 662910

Yore Mill, Aysgarth Falls

Yore Mill, a grade II listed building that was home to the Yorkshire Museum of Carriages, now houses a tea shop and a craft shop, the latter offering a selection of paintings, pottery, models and candles. Website: www.yore-mill.co.uk; Tel: 01969 663496.

West Burton

West Burton is a Dales village about 3 miles from Aysgarth. Head east along the A684 and turn right along the B6160. Burton Force waterfall and Packhorse Bridge add to the charm of this quiet, slightly off the beaten track, place. The green is large and safe for children to play on, while the village pub may attract the adults.

Bolton Castle

See Walk 2.

7. *Middleham*

Middleham is regarded as being the smallest market town in Yorkshire. Its bustling, attractive market square is surrounded by imposing stone buildings. There are numerous cafés.

Middleham Castle ruins are the remains of a classic castle and will be a draw for many children. The town is an important racehorse training place and thoroughbreds are easily to be seen in the town and out in the fields which this walk crosses on its way down to the banks of the cover.

Note: some parts of this walk may be tricky for small children – there is one steep section which may also be muddy.

Starting point: The market place, Middleham (SE 129877)

Distance: 2½ miles (add another half mile if you choose the additional branch to William's Hill)

Terrain: Mostly across pastures, including a riverside section along the banks of the cover. Gentle slopes for the most part though there is quite a steep little section mid-way along the riverside.

Map: OS Explorer OL30 Yorkshire Dales: Northern and Central Areas.

Public Toilets: Middleham

Refreshments: Middleham

Pushchairs: Around the streets of Middleham and along the lane by the Castle would be suitable, though the rest of the walk being on un-made paths limits pushchairs to these areas.

☺ You should pass most of these things on your walk. See how many you can spot.

☐ castle ruins

☐ a moat

☐ a flag

☐ cobbles

☐ a racehorse

☐ a butterfly

☐ buttercups

☐ a ladybird

☐ a hay bale

☐ sheep

☐ an ash tree

☐ stepping stones

From the market place in Middleham walk up the hill, passing the Black Swan on your left, as far as the Castle Keep Tea Room. Turn left along the cobbled lane to pass the castle ruins on your right.

☺ Parts of the castle were built in 1170 – over 800 years ago. Look out for the moat.

A famous historic resident of Middleham Castle was Richard III of Wars of the Roses renown. He lived here before becoming king in

The entrance to Middleham Castle *(Graham Beech)*

1483. Edward IV and Henry VI were both imprisoned here during the Wars of the Roses.

Continue along the track as far as a metal farm gate.

If you want to take the additional option of walking up to William's Hill, the public footpath to take is diagonally off to the right through a stone gap stile, just before you reach the metal farm gate.

William's Hill Earthworks represent the remains of a ring and bailey ancient castle.

From William's Hill return to the metal gate. Beyond the metal gate, press straight ahead to the crest.

There are views down the dale and across as far as Leyburn, as well as back over to the castle.

☺ To the left of the castle you can see one of the stables where racehorses are kept in Middleham. We should pass quite a few of these horses on our walk, if we are lucky.

☺ The Middleham Jewel was found here in the 1980s. This buried treasure is a gold and sapphire pendant. It is 400 years old and was sold for over £2 million.

At the end of the field is a wooden stile to cross into the next field where you should turn sharp right to another stile to cross and turn sharp left. Walk towards a small dales barn with the dry stone wall on your left.

Keep going until there is a stream. Bear left of this to follow the path along the length of a wooded gully. At the bottom, keep the fence on your left until the trodden path leads you gently to the right.

Make your way down to a wood fence with the River Cover beyond.

☺ The River Cover gives its name to Coverdale. We are near the bottom of Coverdale. This joins Wensleydale just 1½ miles from here at the confluence (joining) of the Cover with the Ure – the river of Wensleydale.

To the left is a stile to cross into a hummocky area. Walk along with

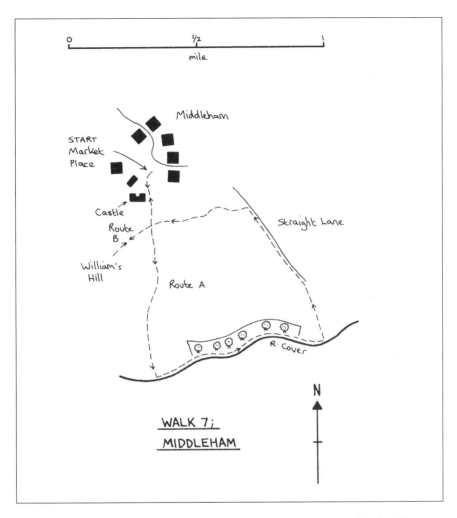

the fence and river on your right. Cross the waymarked stile you reach and continue into the woods beyond.

Keep following the riverside path as it rises quite steeply above the river bank. Coming to a fork, take the right option downhill to a small wooden gate at a distinct river bend.

Through the waymarked gate you enter a field to walk diagonally left towards a straight upward-leading track. Bear right of this, sticking to the lower grassy path at river level.

Continue along the river.

There are stepping stones over the river, but these are not part of the route. They are a right of way however, so you could cross them and return to this bank.

 These stepping stones are believed to be the original ones used by travellers between Middleham Castle and Jervaulx Abbey (2½ miles further downstream) for 800 years.

Come to a stile. Cross it and turn left up the rise. Follow the dry stone wall on your left until you pass through a metal farm gate.

This is Straight Lane.

Follow the lane until it approaches the main road. Before you actually reach the road, turn left through a waymarked gap stile and walk straight ahead with the dry stone wall on your right.

 Ahead of us you can see the ruins of Middleham Castle again, which is where we are going to.

From the top corner of the field, turn left and then right through a waymarked wooden gate. Carry on to a stile and beyond this along the straight and narrow path until you reach its end. Turn right along the track and return to Middleham castle and town.

Other Places of Interest in the Area

Leyburn and the Candle Workshop, Wensley
See Walk 3.

Aysgarth Falls
See Walk 6.

Jervaulx Abbey
This ruined abbey is a Cistercian foundation. The abbey is surrounded by open green spaces and wild flowers abound. You can visit at any time. There is a shop and tea room next to the car park. A fine rather than rainy day attraction for the children. Website: www.jervaulxbbbey.co.uk

8. Ribblehead

The Ribblehead Viaduct is one of the most famous industrial heritage sites in the country. Its 24 arches majestically bestride this moorland site. The juxtaposition of such apparent wilderness with the architectural grandeur of this Victorian colossus is breathtakingly dramatic.

The walk begins in sight of the viaduct and crosses the moorland beneath it before looping back beneath the railway to lead you alongside the track and then back down beside the structure itself. There are opportunities to see the signal box at Bleamoor and Ribblehead Station itself. For the railway-struck child this walk is a must and for the rest of the family a dramatic and thought-provoking experience. This moorland is exposed. The weather can be windy, damp and chilly. Come prepared even in summer, and reflect on the conditions for the 2000 labourers who built the bridge.

Starting point: Ribblehead car park (SD 764792). This lies just before the Station Inn, on the right, as you drive towards the railway from the junction of the B6255 and B6479 at Ribblehead.

Distance: Route A: 2½ miles; Route B: 3¼ miles

Terrain: The first half is on gravel or metalled tracks and relatively easy underfoot. There is some muddy rough pasture to cross for much of the second half.

Map: OS Explorer OL2 Yorkshire Dales: Southern and Western Areas.

Toilets: Ribblehead (Station Inn)

Refreshments: Ribblehead

Pushchairs: In terms of terrain alone the gravel approach to the viaduct and beyond to Gunnerfleet Farm is viable but the strength of wind is off-putting on all but the calmest of summer days.

☺ You should pass most of these things on your walk. See how many you can spot.

☐ a train

☐ a heritage award plaque

☐ a tent

☐ a Victorian smoking a pipe

☐ a black and a white-faced sheep

☐ a metal No. 14 sign

☐ a Dales barn

☐ limestone boulders

☐ a Land Rover

☐ train buffers

☐ a signal box

☐ a waterfall

From the car park follow the broad gravel track up to and underneath the viaduct.

Ribblehead Viaduct *(Graham Beech)*

Q: How many arches does the viaduct have?

A: 24

Stop at the viewing table.

☺ The plaque shows two workers shaking hands across the years. The one on the left represents the people who built the bridge in 1875 and the one on the left the modern-day engineers who restored it in 1991, so that it can still be used by trains today.

☺ On the top are directions to places nearby. Batty Green was where the 2000 workers were housed in the 1870s. There are no buildings there now, but it was once a bustling place of temporary shacks – rather like a town of the American west.

Follow the track beyond the viaduct.

To either side are collapsed shake holes – stay on the track.

☺ Limestone is rock which can react with water so that it is dissolved. Obviously this happens very slowly and only where there are already cracks, or joints, is the effect noticeable, but it can cause the ground to collapse into a hollow – which is what these shakeholes are.

Keep on the track past the buildings of Gunnerfleet Farm, having passed through one farm gate on the way, until you need to go through the gate to cross the bridge over the stream to the metalled lane beyond. Turn right along this.

As you walk along here look out for a limestone boulder field which at first site appears to be standing stones.

☺ Some of these stones look as though people have put them there, but they are completely natural. They are blocks of limestone which have been broken off by the weather and either fallen or been carried to this place by saturated soil which has sunk down the hillside.

Go through the gate to pass by the boulder field and reach a T-junction of lanes. Turn right and cross the stile you reach.

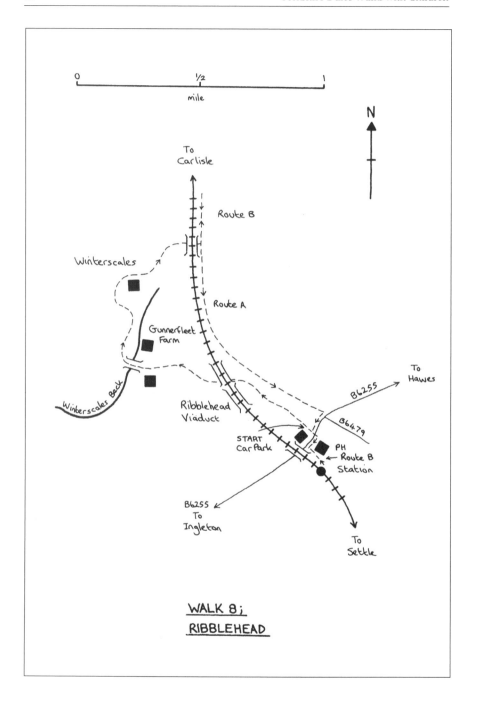

WALK 8;
RIBBLEHEAD

☺ The waymark post here points the way to one of the biggest mountains in the Dales.

Q: Which one?
A: Whernside

☺ Whernside, Pen-y-Ghent and Ingleborough are called the Three Peaks. People come from all over the country to walk up all three. Later on this walk we will probably see some of them.

Just after you pass Winterscales Farm on your left, bear right in the direction indicated Whernside over a small stone bridge.

☺ There is a small waterfall here **(INDICATE LEFT)** where a small tributary stream meets Little Dale Beck to become Winterscales Beck. A confluence is the name given to a place where two streams meet like this.

Walk on to pass between the dry stone wall and a Dales barn to reach and pass through a gate to follow the path up and left. Keep following the stony way.

Ahead, a Victorian signal box (at Bleamoor for the sidings) and home (red and white) signal come into view.

INDICATE THEM.

☺ That wooden building over there is the signal box at Bleamoor. People in the box can work signals like the red and white one we can see to let the trains move or make them stop. If the flag is straight out it means stop, if it is at an angle it means they can go. A red and white signal like that is called a home signal because it is near the signal box. Signals here controlled engines pushing trucks in and out of the sidings here.

The path becomes damper and muddier along here before leading you through a tunnel under the railway.

Route B: **To see the signal box close-to turn left and walk up to it. Then return to this point.**

Route A: **To continue the walk turn right and follow the path**

alongside the railway and then down by the viaduct to rejoin the gravel track back to the car park.

This section of the walk is much used by people walking the Three Peaks. A broad and muddy scar disfigures the moor where countless boots have trodden. There are issues here of how popular walks should be managed in wilderness areas.

☺ You can see where very many people have walked along here. Do you think it looks attractive? What do you think should be done about it?

Possible solutions you could discuss are:

Nothing

Re-route the walk

Construct a path or steps here with a surface that tries to blend in with the scenery

This last solution has been adopted at Malham Cove (walk 19). You could compare that with here if you have already done that walk.

You could also point out that your boots – and mine! – are all adding to the problem.

Route B: You may want to visit the station at Ribblehead. Walk on beyond the car park and turn right then left, as indicated by the signposts. Then return to the car park.

Other Places of Interest in the Area

Dentdale

Drive down Dentdale from Ribblehead (head first along the B6255 towards Hawes and then turn left as signposted) and you will find yourself in a look-alike valley for Postman Pat's Greendale. In Dent itself (Walk 4) you will find a charming little place with white-washed buildings and narrow cobbled streets. There are plentiful shops and refreshment opportunities.

Ingleton Waterfalls

The waterfalls walk, on the fringe of Ingleton village, is a privately run attraction and there is a charge (Tel: 01756 795621). A 4½-mile trail passes five falls including Thornton Force and leads through ancient woodland. There are refreshments available at the car park and in Ingleton village itself which lies at the junction of the A65 from Skipton and B6255 from Hawes. The waterfalls walk is well signposted for miles around.

White Scar Cave

White Scar Cave is an underground attraction (Tel: 01524 241244). An underground waterfall and thousands of stalactites are among the highlights of the tour which takes about an hour and a quarter. The caves are signposted of the B6255 road from Ingleton to Hawes, about 1½ miles from Ingleton. The tour is open every day except Christmas Day and includes hard hats. There are paths and lights throughout. There is a café and picnic area. Website: www.whitescar cave.co.uk

9. *Buckden*

Buckden is a village in Upper Wharfedale. There is a large village green surrounded by a small but varied range of refreshment facilities. On a fine day it is pleasant to picnic there after completing the circular walk which begins and ends at the village car park.

The first section of the walk is very straight. Buckden Rake is in fact an old Roman legion marching route.

Along the way, the walk approaches the banks of the Wharfe on a number of occasions and children may be able to get down to the water's edge.

Starting point: Car park, Buckden (SD 942773)

Distance: 4½ miles

Terrain: The walk begins with a climbing, and then ridge-top, track to Cray. There follows a cross-pasture section to Hubberholme, returning by lane and riverside path

Map: OS Explorer OL30 Yorkshire Dales: Northern and Central Areas.

Public Toilets: Buckden

Refreshments: Buckden, Cray (White Lion), Hubberholme (George Inn)

Pushchairs: Around Buckden village and the lanes in the vicinity of Hubberholme are the pushchair-friendly sections of this walk

---

☺ You should pass most of these things on your walk. See how many you can spot.

☐ a stone bridge

☐ scree

☐ black cattle

☐ an aircraft

☐ a beech tree

☐ a holly bush in a boulder

☐ a waterfall

☐ a confluence of streams

☐ a church tower

☐ a sycamore tree

☐ buttercups

☐ a grasshopper

Leave the car park by the gate at the opposite end from the toilet block. Walk up the track.

Buckden Bridge *(Rebecca Terry)*

☺ This land belongs to the National Trust. They are a charity who look after important parts of our heritage. Sometimes that means old buildings like stately homes. Sometimes, it means parts of the landscape that people think are especially work keeping – like Upper Wharfedale.

To the right limestone screes are visible where rocks loosened from the higher block-jointed limestone have tumbled down the slope.

At the top you pass through a gate and walk on to a fork. Bear left to a gate and continue straight ahead through a wood gate.

Q: What is the symbol carved on this gate?

A: It is the Yorkshire Dales National Park Symbol – a sheep's face

Keep walking along until you pass through successive dry stone wall gaps and reach a wooden hurdle gate with a stone stile to its right. Beyond the gate come to a single gate adjacent to a 3-way marker post. Turn left, through the gate, in the direction of Cray – not Cray Bridge.

Follow the path down to a dry stone wall. Continue the descent, with the dry stone wall on your right.

The building ahead is the White Lion Inn at Cray.

At the bottom of the slope is a waymark post. Turn right and walk on as far as a seven-bar gate. Bear right to the stepping stones and cross them.

The river here is the Wharfe. You can see pot-holes in the river bed here where the Wharfe has swirled stones to drill into the rock floor.

Cross the road by the White Lion.

The White Lion inn is open all day and serves bar meals. It has a car park but notices warn against parking and walking from here.

To the right of the pub, beneath a tree a public footpath sign shows the way.

Q: Where does the sign point to next?

A: Stubbing Bridge

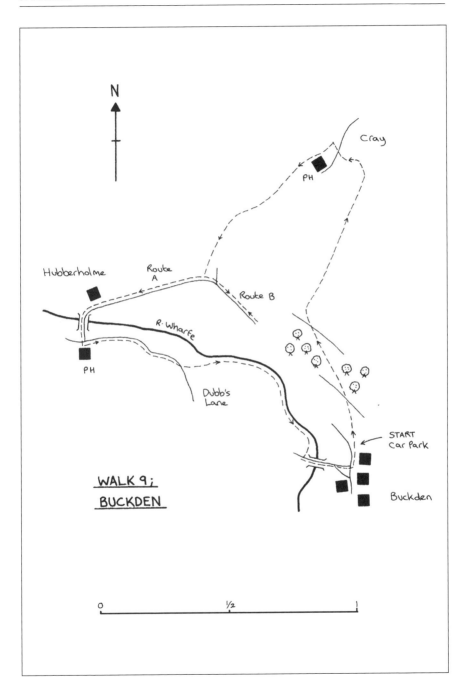

N

Cray

PH

Hubberholme

Route A

Route B

R. Wharfe

PH

Dubb's Lane

START
Car Park

Buckden

WALK 9;
BUCKDEN

0   ½

Follow the path to a waymarker. Bear left just before the post to
join a slightly lower track. Go right and then turn left by the next
waymarker to take up the path to Stubbing Bridge.

Pass through the gate you reach and descend towards the stream
(INDICATE LEFT))

☺ This stream is called Cray Gill. Look out for waterfalls along here.

Continue. Cross the lines of two dry stone walls before bearing
right across a low stone bridge at the confluence of streams. Walk
through the glade and beyond until you reach a ladder stile.

Climb the stile and carry on to reach a six-bar gate leading onto the
surfaced lane. Turn right along the lane.

Escape route: Turn left to walk up to the junction with Buckden Wood
Lane and then turn right to walk alongside the road back to Buckden.

The lane brings you to Hubberholme.

When the buildings of Hubberholme become visible ahead on the
right, point them out.

The stone buildings there are Hubberholme. On the left here is a flood
gauge which people can use to see how high the river is rising if there is a
risk of flooding after heavy rain.

The church of St Michael and All Angels at Hubberholme dates back in
part to the thirteenth century.

Cross the bridge over the Wharfe. Turn left again to the George Inn
and left again to follow the surfaced Dubb's Lane.

The George Inn is the venue for the annual meeting of the almost a
thousand year old local parliament on New Year's day.

☺ This part of our walk is along the Dales Way which is a
long-distance footpath wandering around many of the dales in the
National Park. It runs the length of Wharfedale – all the way from
Ilkley by way of Bolton Abbey. The whole path is 84 miles (135km)
long and eventually goes to Bowness in the Lake District.

Turn left to follow the Dales Way along the banks of the Wharfe as waymarked to Buckden Bridge by an eight-bar gate. This is after you have passed Grange Farm on the right.

Follow the Dales Way, crossing three wooden stiles on the way to Buckden Bridge. Pass through the gate and turn left to cross into Buckden village and walk back to the car park.

Other Places of Interest in the Area

Upper Wharfedale Museum – Grassington

Grassington is a bustling Dales town with a lot of tourist enterprises. You won't be short of shops, cafés, pubs, ice creams and so on. There are quieter corners to explore too, however, and the Upper Wharfedale Museum, on the market place, is a small but interesting indoor venue open afternoons from April to September (Tel: 01756 752801).

Bolton Abbey

Bolton Abbey (Walk 20) lies just north of the A59 Harrogate to Skipton road. It is the Yorkshire estate of the Duke and Duchess of Devonshire. Apart from the ruined 12th-century priory, there are nature trails, riverside picnic sites and a variety of refreshment outlets along a 3½-mile stretch of the River Wharfe known as the Strid. The Strid car park, north of the main priory one, is the beginning of a special children's trail. Bolton Abbey is open all year (Tel: 01756 718009). Website: www.boltonabbey.co.uk

Aysgarth Falls

See Walk 5.

10. Fountains Abbey

Fountains Abbey is a world heritage site off the B6265 Ripon to Pateley Bridge road. It is well signposted. It was founded in the twelfth century by monks from York – originally just thirteen of them. It is the most complete Cistercian remain in Britain.

The abbey and grounds are run by the National Trust (website: www.fountainsabbey.co.uk). There is an admission charge of £7.50 per adult and £4 per child (2007 prices). Family admission is £20 (worth it with 2 adults and 2 children). National Trust members have free admission. The child-friendliness of the facility, particularly for babies and small toddlers, is however exceptional which is why I have exceptionally included a walk which is not free.

The entire route can be done with a pushchair. There are parent and baby rooms with nappy change facilities at the Visitor Centre. For a family's first venture out with a new arrival, this is the walk you want. Because it is in the abbey grounds, opportunities to short-cut or pick and choose parts of the walk are many.

Starting point: Fountains Abbey Visitor Centre

Distance: 3 miles approx. for the full route

Terrain: The walk is nearly all on prepared paths (and can be entirely so if you choose) and otherwise is across the flat, mown grass of the grounds around the ruins. There is a significant descent down to, and back from the ruins – on prepared paths.

Map: Obtainable from the visitor centre. Children's guides may also be purchased there. OS Explorer Map 298: Nidderdale.

Public Toilets: Fountains Abbey Visitor Centre and by the lake

Pushchairs: The whole walk is very suitable for pushchairs

☺ You should pass most of these things on your walk. See how many you can spot.

☐ a pheasant

☐ an oak tree

☐ a conker

☐ a beech tree

☐ a temple

☐ a green face in a window

☐ a duck

☐ some stepping stones

☐ a feather

☐ a mushroom (don't pick it!)

☐ a pond shaped like the Moon

☐ an angel

Begin at the visitor centre admissions hall exit. Bear left and follow the curving path through 2 sets of wooden gates.

☺ As we go along here look out for the top of the Abbey tower coming into view.

Turn sharp right, with the path, and follow it gently downhill to a black metal gate. Go through and turn left to descend more steeply.

In front of the ruins, turn right and walk down to the junction of pathways. Turn left and cross the grass to the ruins.

☺ Fountains Abbey was mostly built between 850 and 750 years ago, although the tower was not added until 450 years ago, so it is much younger than the rest. It has been a ruin for 400 years (so the tower didn't last very long!).

Walk up the nave.

☺ Look out along here for the red and yellow stone in the columns.

At the end of the nave, turn right through an arch.

Fountains Abbey *(Rebecca Terry)*

Before doing so have a look at the left-hand end windows. The last window has two figures – an angel and a Green Man (a medieval fertility symbol).

☺ Look up at the end window. You can see an angel and a strange looking face with branches called a Green Man.

Look out here for a small flight of "secret" steps just to the left of the arch which emerge at the top of the ruined wall on the other side. However, do not send a child up these – there is a sudden drop on the other side. You could surprise them by your sudden appearance.

Walk ahead and turn left at the T-junction of pathways.

Walk freely across the grass to join the cliff foot prepared path and walk along that, with the river on your right.

☺ The river here is the River Skell.

Keep on going until the path curves lengthily and steeply left and you come to a junction of paths.

Short-cut: Turn right here across the rustic bridge and then right again

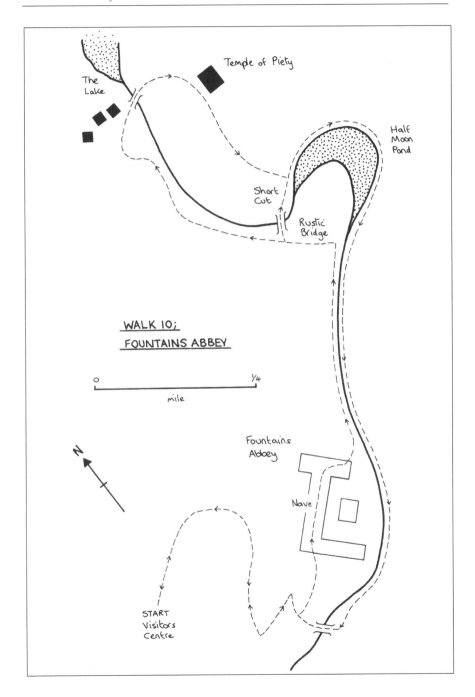

The Lake

Temple of Piety

Half Moon Pond

Short Cut

Rustic Bridge

WALK 10;
FOUNTAINS ABBEY

0 ¼
mile

N

Fountains Abbey

Nave

START
Visitors
Centre

along the far bank of the River Skell. You will have re-joined the main
route at the Half Moon Pond.

**Carry on straight ahead if you are not taking the short-cut until you
reach a fork. Bear right and continue until you are approaching the
gilded gates by the lake.**

At the lake is a good half-way resting point. There are toilets, the
Studley tea room and picnic tables. The lake is thronged by ducks and
water fowl.

**Turn right to cross the bridge or stepping stones over the canal by
the cascade, and then head to the right.**

☺ The pools on the right make up the Moon Pond and its crescents.

☺ The stone building we are going to pass is the Temple of Piety. It
was built in the 1740s.

**Where the short-cut path across the rustic bridge re-joins from the
right, continue past the Half Moon Pond on your right. Then keep
to the path by the water all the way back to the ruins where it rises
to the left before swinging down and right to return you to the foot
of the descent from the visitors centre.**

Turn left and climb back up to the visitor centre.

Other Places of Interest in the Area

Ripon

The market and minster town of Ripon is on the eastern periphery of
the Dales region, just three miles from Fountains. There are lots of
shops and refreshment places here and its bustling atmosphere on
Saturday and Thursday (market day) is in marked contrast to the
tranquillity of the Abbey.

Pateley Bridge

A linear, one-main-street town at the southern end of Nidderdale,
Pateley Bridge is a good base camp for exploring that valley. There is
a range of shops, cafés and meal-serving pubs and the Nidderdale

Museum (open daily from Easter to September, Tel 01423 711225). Nidderdale Show is held in the town in late September.

Ripley Castle

Ripley Castle lies south of Ripon, off the A61 Harrogate Road. The Castle has been altered over the centuries to resemble more a castellated stately home than the turreted fortress of a child's imagination. Inside, however, are secret passages and collections of old armaments as well as furniture. Fine grounds surround the castle and are home to the National Hyacinth Collection and a collection of tropical plants. The castle is open every day in July and August and on some days in other months. It may be as well to check – on 01423 770152. Website: www.ripleycastle.co.uk.

11. Middlesmoor and How Stean Gorge

Middlesmoor is in Upper Nidderdale and is the most northerly Nidderdale village, being the end of the line so far as its access road is concerned. The cobbled back streets of the village are especially pretty in spring when crocus, daffodil and snowdrops are in flower.

How Stean Gorge is known as "Yorkshire's Little Switzerland". The gorge was carved out during the Ice Age and reaches depths up to 24 metres (80 feet).

Starting point: Middlesmoor car park (SE 093743) is to be found by driving right through the village, beyond the Crown Hotel.

Distance: Route A: 2½ miles; Route B: 3 miles

Terrain: Mostly over pasture fields, generally straightforward going with a bit if a pull up to Middlesmoor church at the end

Map: OS Explorer OL30 Yorkshire Dales: Northern and Central Areas.

Public Toilets: Middlesmoor

Refreshments: Middlesmoor, How Stean Gorge, Lofthouse

Pushchairs: This is not a pushchair route

☺ You should pass most of these things on your walk. See how many you can spot.

☐ *a cockerel*

☐ *a dry stone wall*

☐ *a church clock*

☐ *a Dales barn*

☐ *an oak tree*

☐ *a saw mill*

☐ *a rose hip*

☐ *a peacock*

☐ *a dry stone wall*

☐ *a hen*

☐ *a lamb*

☐ *holly*

Turn left out of the car park entrance and walk down into the village. Keep going down the steep hill out of the village and round the leftward hairpin bend. Turn right through the stone stile on your right.

There is a Dales barn opposite.

☺ These stone barns (Dales barns) are a feature of the countryside here. Farmers use them for storage and animals can shelter in them in bad weather.

Walk along the edge of the pasture, keeping the hedgerow on your right. Pass through the waymarked gap stile you reach and continue, dry stone wall to your right.

On the other side of the dale the hamlet of Stean is visible.

☺ The small settlement over there is called Stean. It is a hamlet rather than a village. Hamlets are usually smaller than villages, often without shops. However, the crucial difference is that a village has a church, but a hamlet does not.

Q: What does that make Middlesmoor?

A: A village.

Pass through the next stone gap stile and again continue to a Nidderdale way waymark post. Do not pass through this stile, but bear left to head for the lower of two metal gates on the other side of the field.

☺ The trees over to the right **(INDICATE)** are growing in How Stean Gorge which we are soon going to see. It is a very narrow, deep valley cut in the rock. We will be walking over a footbridge across it.

Go through the lower gate and walk straight across the next pasture, again to the lower of two gates. Go through this and walk on to pass through the next gate, beside a Dales barn.

☺ Here is another of those barns, like we saw near the start.

Q: Can you remember what they are called?
A: Dales barns

Right to the next waymarked gate. Make straight for the car park.

☺ This car park is for How Stean Gorge. There is a café here. (there is also an adventure playground). Some people drive their cars here just for that and to visit the gorge and its caves.

How Stean Gorge Café sells ice creams. It offers a range of meals including vegetarian options and children's portions. Visits to the caves are supported by the loan of helmets and hire of torches from the café.

Cross the red-railed footbridge.

☺ The ravine is up to 80 feet (24 metres) deep.

Walk out of the car park's white gates onto the minor road. Turn left.

This lane is part of the Nidderdale Way.

☺ This part of the walk is along a section of the Nidderdale Way. We saw a sign for it earlier, if you remember, when we were crossing the fields from Middlesmoor. The Nidderdale Way is a long distance footpath right round Nidderdale.

Middlesmoor church *(Graham Beech)*

☺ Looking over the wall to our left along here, we can see the gorge quite clearly.

Follow the road as it bends sharply left to cross the gorge. Continue along the road to a junction.

☺ Over there **(INDICATE LEFT)** is the church at Middlesmoor where we will finish our walk.

Escape route: Turn left and walk back to Middlesmoor.

Bear right and continue in the direction of Lofthouse as far as a marked right-hand bend.

Route A: There are two kissing gates here – either side of a red metal gate. Go through the one on the left.

Route B: continue along the road, turning left into Lofthouse to see the village and perhaps avail yourself of its refreshment facilities. Turn left again across the bridge over the Nidd to return to this point.

Walk up the pasture towards a Dales barn. There is a dry stone

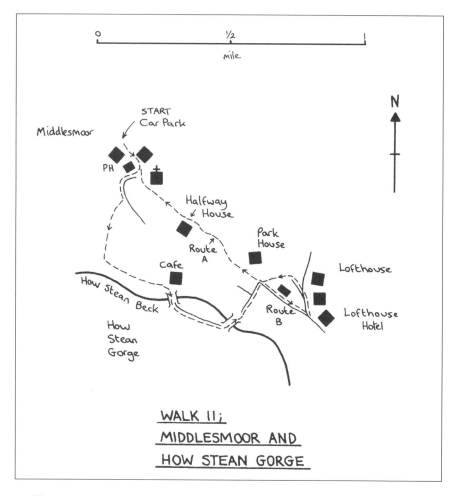

WALK 11;
MIDDLESMOOR AND
HOW STEAN GORGE

wall on your right. Follow the wall beyond the barn until you reach
a gap. Cross it and bear left, keeping the dry stone wall on your
left.

☺ Look back at the way we have been walking. There is a good view
down Nidderdale from here.

Q: What is the name of the river which Nidderdale is named after?
A: The River Nidd

Ahead are three mature trees.

Walk ahead and see if you can tell which of the three trees ahead is an oak tree.

It is the first.

Make for some steps ahead. These take you over the wall into the next pasture. Follow the path, then track towards Halfway House.

 The building ahead is Halfway House. It is about halfway between Lofthouse and Middlesmoor.

At Halfway House pass through the single, wood, waymarked gate and bear right between the older stone buildings and the modern byre. Take the left of two gates (it is waymarked) out of the far end of the yard and follow the dry stone wall on your right.

Head straight up the hill towards Middlesmoor church, passing through a stone gap stile, and ascending a flight of steps to reach the white gate at the top. Walk along the stone-flagged path and turn left down the cobbled street you encounter. At the end of this, turn right to the car park beyond the Crown Hotel.

Other Places of Interest in the Area

Stump Cross Caverns

An underground and therefore wet weather attraction, Stump Cross Caverns are a limestone cave system where the visitor can see numerous stalactites and stalagmites as well as other lit, weird and wonderful rock formations. There are paths throughout and guided tours are conducted. The caverns are open to the public daily between mid-March and mid-November (Tel 01756 752780). A shop sells mineral specimens. Website: www.stumpcrosscaverns.co.uk.

Brimham Rocks

These fantastically-shaped millstone grit rocks stand 6 metres tall on Nidderdale Moor. They are products of natural weathering. A National Trust site, Brimham Hall acts as information and refreshment centre (Tel 01423 770584) for the rocks which are to be found 4 miles east of Pateley Bridge, off the B6265 road to Ripon

Pateley Bridge

See Walk 10.

12. Horton in Ribblesdale

Horton in Ribblesdale is an upland Dales village with a strong Pennine feel. Serious outdoorists, often heading off to tackle Pen-Y-Ghent and the other two of the three peaks – Whernside and Ingleborough, as well as the much less ambitious, are among its visitors. Our route is a gentle one across valley floor fields, taking in the banks of the Ribble.

Horton in Ribblesdale has a station on the famous Settle-Carlisle railway which crosses the nearby, spectacular, Ribblehead Viaduct (walk 8). You may like to combine your walk with a ride on this. Do, however, check times in advance with the Tourist Information Centre in Horton (01729 860333) or in Settle (01729 825192).

Starting point: Horton in Ribblesdale car park (SD 807727)

Distance: 2 miles

Terrain: The walk begins by leading you through the village and then out across pastureland to return by a riverside path to Horton.

Map: OS Explorer OL2 Yorkshire Dales: Southern and Western Areas.

Public Toilets: Horton in Ribblesdale

Refreshments: Horton in Ribblesdale

Pushchairs: The lanes around Horton itself would really be the limit of pushchairability.

☺ You should pass most of these things on your walk. See how many you can spot.

☐ a mountain biker

☐ an old-style telephone box

☐ a tourist information office

☐ a church tower

☐ dry stone walls

☐ a quarry

☐ a train

☐ a sheep with blue marking

☐ a Land Rover

☐ ducks

☐ rapids

☐ water between planks

The Ribble at Horton *(Graham Beech)*

Starting from the car park, turn right along the street.

On a clear day you will be able to see Pen-Y-Ghent (694m) to your left.

☺ Look over there **(INDICATE LEFT)** and you can see a mountain
called Pen-y-Ghent. It is nearly 700m above sea-level (that's
about 2300 feet). This road is about 240m above sea-level so the
mountain top is about 450m higher than us.

**At the corner by the Golden Lion Hotel, walk straight on down
Chapel Lane and the succeeding walled farm lane until you have
passed two complete fields on your right. Turn right across the
small stone stile to cross the ladder stile on the field boundary over
to your left.**

**Join the farm track, walking to your right. When the track
suddenly turns across the stream, go straight ahead along the
narrow, trodden pathway.**

**Follow the direction indicated by a waymark post over a small
footbridge. Walk round the side of the pasture, keeping the trees to
your right until you approach the large new footbridge over the
Ribble.**

Pass through the metal gate and cross the bridge.

☺ Down to the left here is a ford. The farmer may use this to drive
farm equipment through the shallow river. This new bridge saves
us getting our feet wet!

☺ On the right there are some large boulders which the river has left
here. After heavy rain there will be more water in the river than
today and these boulders will be moved along.

**Straight ahead the railway line is evident. Settle is along to the left
and Horton, the Ribblehead Viaduct and, ultimately Carlisle, are
to the north and right.**

At the end of the bridge is a waymark post.

Q: Which way is it back to Horton?
A: To the right. Left would take us to Helwith Bridge.

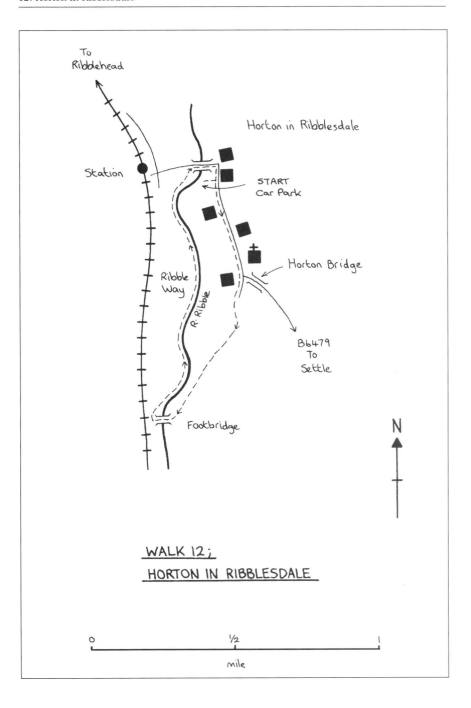

To
Ribblehead

Station

Horton in Ribblesdale

START
Car Park

Horton Bridge

Ribble
Way

R. Ribble

B6479
To
Settle

Footbridge

N

WALK 12;

HORTON IN RIBBLESDALE

0   ½   1

mile

Walk to the right and along the river bank. Cross a ladder stile and small footbridge en-route.

At the river meander it is possible to see where the river cliff has been protected from further erosion by large stones.

Q: What have we walked over that suggests the soil may have been partly washed away by the river in flood?

A: Exposed tree roots.

☺ Look over to the other bank and you can see where boulders have been place to protect the bank over there. It is on the outside of the bend, so erosion is more powerful there. You can also see a confluence where a small tributary stream joins the Ribble.

Continue on the riverside path.

This is part of the Ribble Way long distance path.

☺ There are some special waymark signs to look out for along here because this is part of the Ribble Way. See if you can find one.

The Ribble Way markers show a logo in which the letters RW are made to look like flowing water.

As the pasture on your left narrows and you come very near to a dry stone walled lane on your left look out for a waymarked right turn through the hedgerow and back to the river bank. Then turn left to walk alongside the Ribble again.

After crossing a couple of stiles and pastures you will find that, for a short stretch, the path is atop a low wall. At the end you need to clamber left over a rock to access the single path ahead.

At the waymark post turn right through a low gate and down the ladder stile. Follow the path ahead, over a stile, along the riverside as far as the bridge. Cross the stile here and go up the steps to the bridge.

Q: How many steps are there and what does the RW stand for?

A: 6 and Ribble Way

At the time of writing the footbridge here is being renewed. If it is restored by the date of your walk use it instead of the road bridge described. You will emerge at the car park.

Turn right to cross the next bridge and walk up to the car park.

Other Places of Interest in the Area

Settle

The busy market town of Settle (Walk 18) is in Ribblesdsale. The market square with its shambles arcade and quaint back streets and yards make it an especially attractive place to wander. There is a wealth of cafés and eateries, including the famous Ye Olde Naked Man. Market day is Tuesday.

The Museum of North Craven life and the Watershed Mill Craft Centre (Tel 01729 822361) on Langcliffe Road, which features children's art activity, are possible points of interest for children. So too is the Horse's Health Farm at nearby Rathmell, just off the A65, to the west. Here visitors can see horses swimming and enjoying solarium treatment. The health farm is open from the end of May to September (Tel 01729 840284).

Ribblehead Viaduct

See Walk 8.

Clapham and Ingleborough Cave

See Walk 15.

13. *Litton*

As the name might suggest, Litton is in Littondale. One of the lesser known Yorkshire Dales. This is a tributary of the much larger Wharfedale, joining the latter between Kettlewell and Conistone. Litton itself is a linear village with the Queen's Arms inn at its eastern end being the first noticeable building if you drive up the dale from Wharfedale.

The walk takes you down and across the River Skirfare by two ford crossings. In dry weather you will not even have wet feet, but following substantial rain, or outside the summer period, you may do well to check the likely water level in advance, for example by contacting the Tourist Information Office at Grassington National Park Centre (01756 752774). Although relatively short, this is not an undemanding little walk. The terrain is not all easy going and solid footwear will be needed. It is a walk to appeal to the more adventurous, "let's go and explore" child. The route is quite intricate, so the pathfinding youngster will be well employed.

Starting point: Litton Bridge (SD 905742). The minor road running through the village crosses a stream at this bridge.

Distance: 2 miles

Terrain: Across pasture fields from Litton to the banks of the Skirfare, returning by a mixture of pasture and stony riverside path

Map: OS Explorer OL30 Yorkshire Dales: Northern and Central Areas.

Toilets: Litton (Queens Arms)

Refreshments: Litton (Queens Arms)

Pushchairs: Although short, this walk's terrain does not lend itself to pushchairing.

☺ You should pass most of these things on your walk. See how many you can spot.

☐ dry stone walls

☐ black and white cows

☐ a sycamore tree

☐ a water tub

☐ ferns

☐ a rabbit burrow

☐ a butterfly

☐ a sheep with blue marking

☐ a bluebell

☐ a ford

☐ thistles

☐ exposed tree roots

☐ an ash tree

Begin at the bridge and walk down the road in an easterly direction to pass the post office on your right and the Queens Arms on your left.

Turn right in the direction of the River Skirfare through a waymarked gap in the dry stone wall.

The Skirfare is often dry in summer at least so the ford crossing indicated is not a problem. However, out of season, or following wet weather you may be as well to seek local or tourist office advice about water levels first.

Cross the field diagonally and then pass through a waymarked gap stile and wooden gate in quick succession, leading on to a narrow footpath which soon opens out into a green lane.

Bear left of a metal gate to cross a wooden stile and continue along the rest of the green lane, through a six-bar wooden gate into a pasture.

☺ The sign here says we have to keep to the edge of the pasture by the side of the wall. This is so walkers do not damage the grass which the animals need to eat.

Bear right around the edge of the field until you cross a stone stile – the first of a pair. After the second, continue along the green lane. Beyond a third tree, carry straight ahead past a water tub until you reach a further stile.

Cross the stile and bear left as indicated. Cross the next ladder stile and continue down the green lane beyond to the next waymarker where you turn right down the green lane to cross a further stile to the side of the River Skirfare.

☺ The river here is called the Skirfare. Like Wensleydale, Littondale takes the name of a village rather than its river. Wharfedale on the other hand is named after its river.

If your children are familiar with dale names, you might try naming them and deciding if they have rivers of the same names or not. The river in Wensleydale is the Ure.

The Skirfare flows over limestone. It often dries up, because the water soaks into the bed. However, the rounded cobbles which are here can be picked up and carried along by the river when it is flowing.

Follow the path until it takes you to the dry stream bed. Keep walking along with the Skirfare on your right until the path takes you to cross over by means of the ford where the bed is a flat platform of rock.

On the other side, turn left initially and then right as signposted to a small wooden gate. Go through and follow the fence-line on your right.

Follow the grassy track and cross a stile and then a small bridge as you follow the waymarked path to a pair of red metal gates. Pass through the one on the right and walk along with the Skirfare on your right.

At the end is a wooden gate to pass through before the path bears left to the corner of a dry stone wall.

☺ The farm ahead is called East Garth, but we will be turning off before then, so look out for the waymark post we need.

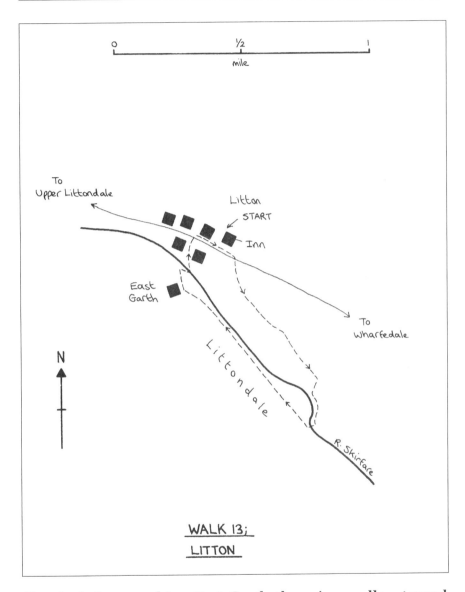

WALK 13;
LITTON

Shortly before reaching East Garth there is a yellow-topped waymark post where you turn right to walk towards a metal gate which gives onto a stony farm track. Turn right along this to the ford crossing. Go over and turn left along the lane.

☺ Along here is a flood gauge so that people can tell how fast the river level is rising when there is a risk of flooding.

If you are here when the river is dry the flood gauge will come as a surprise, but illustrates well how quickly nature can change.

After the lane has bent to the right, follow the bridleway to the right along the walled track and follow round the right-angled left corner. Walk up to the road. The Queens Arms is opposite, the post office and bridge to the left.

The Queen's Arms *(Graham Beech)*

Other Places of Interest in the Area

Kilnsey Park and Trout Farm, Conistone
See Walk 16.

Grassington
See Walk 17.

Bolton Abbey
See Walk 9.

14. Wath in Nidderdale

Wath is a tiny settlement on the right bank of the River Nidd in Upper Nidderdale, a couple of miles to the north of Pateley Bridge

The Sportsman's Arms hotel is the slightly upmarket inn which is the refreshment base for this walk. Bar meals are available, and there is a restaurant.

Starting point: Bridge over the Nidd, Wath in Nidderdale (SE 144677). There is a car park adjacent to the bridge, on the opposite bank to Wath itself.

Distance: Route A: 2¾ miles; Route B: 5 miles

Terrain: Substantially on pasture and lane, with some steep slopes. On Route B the walk includes the crossing of a steep-sided stream valley at mid-way Hillend which is potentially very slippery and may be best reserved for older children.

Map: OS Explorer Map 298: Nidderdale

Toilets: Wath In Nidderdale at the Sportsman's, or else Pateley Bridge.

Refreshments: Wath (Sportsman's Arms)

Pushchairs: Only Grange Lane and the lane to the north of Foster Beck are really suitable.

☺ You should pass most of these things on your walk. See how many
you can spot.

☐ a dry stone wall

☐ a lamb

☐ a tractor

☐ a stable door

☐ a cockerel

☐ a hay bale

☐ a Land Rover

☐ an oak tree

☐ a signpost with a roundel (metal circle) on top

☐ a Dales barn

☐ caravans

☐ a bluebell

**From the roadside car park at Wath Bridge, cross the road to pass
through the waymarked stone gap stile opposite and walk up the
steep grassy bank.**

☺ Look at the Post Box next to the path.

Q: Where do the letters go from here to be delivered?

A: Harrogate

**At the top of the grass bank pass through a gap in the dry stone wall
and then through the next which is to the left of a Dales barn. Walk
straight across the pasture to the top of the rise. From here you can
see the opposite wall with waymarked stile. Pass over and bear left
to mount the slope.**

On the way up here are good views over the Gouthwaite reservoir, up
Nidderdale and over Wath itself.

**The next stile is clear ahead, between a group of conifers to the
right and a single deciduous tree to the left. Cross this and continue
up and towards an oak tree. Beyond, two single gates come into
view; aim for the left one. Cross the waymarked stile.**

Follow the waymarked path round the right-hand edge of the field and through a waymarked gate to pass a series of three small pens and emerge onto the gravel farm track.

☺ Go ahead to the end of the track and see if you can find out the name of this farm.

This is Spring Hill farm.

Turn left along the track and then right onto the minor road. Walk on and turn left along the public bridleway towards Mosscarr and pass Leng Boys Brigade hostel on your left. Continue along the lane as it bends left behind the hostel to reach a cattle grid and a waymark post.

Q: Where does the post indicate?
A: Mosscarr and it says Nidderdale Way.

☺ The Nidderdale Way is a long distance footpath which winds along the dale. We will be following parts of it today.

Walk straight on, not turning right as the track does. Pass through the waymarked left-hand gate of a pair and then bear right. Walk

The approach road to Wath *(Graham Beech)*

on and pass through a green metal gate next and then, after crossing another pasture, aim for two gates ahead.

😊 Go on ahead and see if you can work out which gate we should pass through.

It is the right-hand one because this is waymarked public bridleway.

Follow the dry stone wall on your left to a further gate to pass through. Beyond this, follow the farm track ahead and then turn right behind the modern farm buildings of spring house. At the end of these, bear left, as waymarked, to the first of two black metal gates.

Across the farmyard, follow the tall hedge on your left as far as a spring.

😊 Springs are places where water that is underground comes out onto the ground surface, often starting a stream. What often happens is that a rock which can hold water, such as limestone, has a layer of impervious (waterproof) rock beneath it. The water cannot sink down, so it comes out onto the ground.

Keep the stream to your left and walk down to the surfaced lane alongside Foster Beck.

😊 In the beck are some quite large boulders. When the river is in spate – that means full of water – after heavy rain, or when snow has just melted, these boulders will be carried along by it. You can see that they have become rounded by wearing against each other and against the banks and bed of Foster Beck as they have been carried here.

Route A: Turn left and walk along to the point where the bridleway from Mosscarr joins via a footbridge from the right. There is a green metal gate at this convergence of Routes A and B.

Route B: Turn right.

Turn left at Low Wood, over the footbridge, to join the farm track and follow it round to a gate next to a stone out-building. Go through the gate and then leave the track to follow the dry stone wall on the right, bearing just left of a corner, towards three trees.

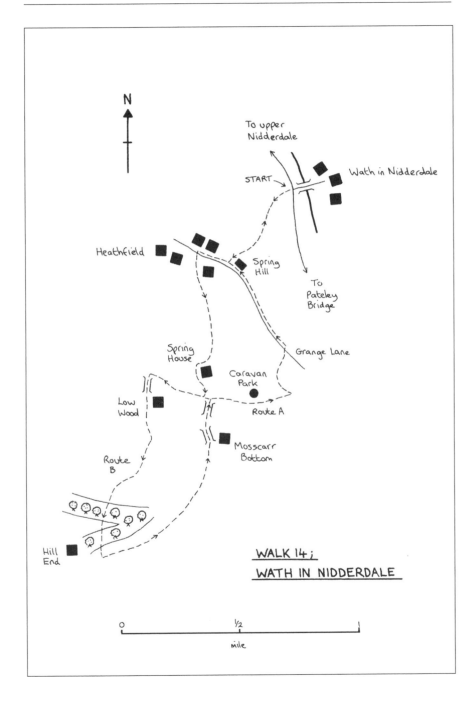

N

To upper
Nidderdale

START

Wath in Nidderdale

Heathfield

Spring
Hill

To
Pateley
Bridge

Grange Lane

Spring
House

Caravan
Park

Low
Wood

Route A

Route
B

Mosscarr
Bottom

Hill
End

WALK 14;
WATH IN NIDDERDALE

0   ½
mile

Re-join the farm track and follow it right until it brings you to a
Dales barn. Pass this and turn left alongside a dry stone wall. At the
corner is a stile. Bear left through this and then turn right to walk
alongside the wall on your right to a farm track.

Turn left onto the track and walk downhill, rounding a hairpin
bend.

Over the wall is a steep and wooded valley.

☺ Look over the wall and see if you can spot a footbridge down there.
That is where we are going.

Find a gap stile through this wall, before you reach the farm gate.

*There are actually two gaps, the first is better. The other side of the
second stile is steep and children will need to be supervised over it.*

Follow the path down to the footbridge and cross over to follow the
path as it emerges from, and then re-enters the woodland via gaps
in the dry stone walls. Cross two stone stiles and the little bridge
and keep on the path until you see a surfaced lane ahead, lined by a
dry stone wall.

A small white gate leads you onto the lane. Turn left along the
Nidderdale Way until the countryside becomes more open and a
stone farm cottage lies ahead. At the second curve of a double bend
in the lane, you should strike off to the left and follow the diagonal
grass path until you reach a dry stone wall.

Join the farm track and walk left to a fork. Bear right, keeping the
dry stone wall on your right, passing through the gateway straight
ahead of you. Keep the wall on your right all the way down to
Mosscarr Bottom.

Go through the red metal gate and take a left to cross the narrow
footbridge. Turn briefly right before following the green lane as it
sweeps left, dry stone walls to either side.

☺ Lanes like this, which are as wide as some minor roads, and are
fenced just as they would be, but are not surfaced are called green
lanes. In many parts of the country they are literally green –
covered by grass. In the Dales they can be too, but are often more

stony, especially where there is limestone, because the soil is not developed enough to allow the grass the grow well.

At the end of the lane, bear right and down towards the caravans. Go through the gate and cross the bridge. This is Foster Beck again.

Routes A and B have now converged.

☺ You may remember this stream from earlier – the one with the boulders.

Q: Do you remember its name?

A: Foster Beck

Turn right along the metalled lane and keep going through the caravan site until you have passed the stone buildings of Heathfield caravan park on your left.

Q: When was this building constructed?

A: 1855 – there is a date on the building.

At the junction, head left, almost back on yourself, but uphill between stone buildings and up a flight of steps. Keep going straight ahead and you will reach a farm gate.

Exit the caravan site via this gate. Walk across the pasture making for the diagonally opposite corner. Go through the gate and walk right to another which gives access onto the metalled grange lane.

Walk up Grange Lane until you reach Spring Hill and turn right to re-trace your early steps back to Wath Bridge.

☺ Keep a look-out for where we parked the car and for Wath itself on the way back down.

Other Places of Interest in the Area

Pateley Bridge

See Walk 10.

Upper Nidderdale

See Walks 11 and 16.

Stump Cross caverns

See Walk 11.

15. Clapham

Clapham is a very pretty Dales village with cottages set either side of a babbling brook – Clapham Beck. As well as the walk described here there is a nature trail in the grounds of Ingleborough Hall and Ingleborough Cave is nearby. Guided tours of the cave include probably the longest stalactite in Britain (1.5 metres).

The area is a popular tourist destination: there are plentiful cafés and pubs serving bar meals in Clapham

---

Starting Point: Clapham National Park Centre (SD 745693)

Distance: 4 miles

Terrain: Mostly over fields which can be muddy, returning along stony Thwaite Lane.

Map: OS Explorer OL2 Yorkshire Dales: Southern and Western Areas.

Public Toilets: Clapham and Austwick

Refreshments: Clapham and Austwick

Pushchairs: Apart from the village itself, little could be successfully attempted by pushchair.

☺ You should pass most of these things on your walk. See how many you can spot:

☐ a sheep with blue marking
☐ a pond
☐ a horse chestnut tree
☐ a limestone boulder
☐ a seat with a carved name
☐ a black-faced sheep
☐ a kestrel

☐ an ash tree

☐ a house named after a tree

☐ a bell

☐ a 4-wheel drive vehicle

☐ scree

By the toilet block of the National Park Centre, a waymark post points you on the way to Austwick – down an initially surfaced path towards the back of the car park and between it and a farm to the right.

Keep going to a waymark post beyond the farmyard and on through the metal kissing gate.

☺ Metal railings and gates like the ones along here are typical of large privately owned estates. This is part of the grounds of Ingleborough Hall, but the path we are on is a public right of way which means that anyone can use it.

At the end of the field are three deciduous trees.

Those three trees ahead are deciduous which means that they shed their leaves in winter.

Q: Which of the three is a horse chestnut?

A: The one on the right.

Pass through the kissing gate and continue to a seat you can see ahead on the left.

☺ Go ahead and see if you can find out what it says on that seat.

The seat is in memory of James Anson Farrer.

☺ Farrer is the name of the family from Ingleborough Hall.

Go on past the next two kissing gates and across pastures to pass a small quarry working on your left.

The ground is noticeably less muddy along here. The soil is drier because the underlying rock is now limestone which is permeable, allowing better drainage. The land use has simultaneously changed from cattle to sheep grazing because the pasture is now less lush.

Notice the rock boulders around here. They are limestone. Limestone lets water pass through it and, because the rain can soak through better here, the path is drier than before.

Cross the stone stile you reach and carry straight on to the next. Cross it too and then walk straight on across the field – not keeping to the wall on your right. Make for and cross the ladder stile over the opposite field boundary. Repeat this at the next wall and then pass a copse of mixed trees on your right.

Q: What tree types can you spot in the copse?
A: Species include ash and sycamore.

Immediately beyond the copse follow the path down to the right and to the next stone stile. Cross this and continue along the path to pass a young tree by a seat.

Walk on to climb the next ladder stile.

The buildings here are in Austwick. There is a shop and a pub here, as well as public toilets. Austwick won the Dalesman 'Best Kept Village In The Dales' award in 1981. The Dalesman, incidentally, is a magazine about the Yorkshire Dales which has been published in Clapham since 1939.

 We are just coming up to Austwick now. This village is the turning point on our walk. We will walk back to Clapham along a lane called Thwaite Lane.

On the other side of the stile the path goes straight ahead and then drops to the road just to the right of a white-walled bungalow.

Turn left alongside the road and keep going past the post office on your right and the Game Cock Inn and primary school on your left.

The school was built by the Inglebys in 1842. There is a stone to this effect above the door.

 Find out who built the school and when.

Go on as far as Townhead Lane. Turn left along this. Walk up the hill, passing Preston's garage on the left, until you reach Victoria Lodge to the right of a left bend. Ignore the footpath which leads off to the right here and continue up the hill past Woodland Heights on the left until you reach a ladder stile.

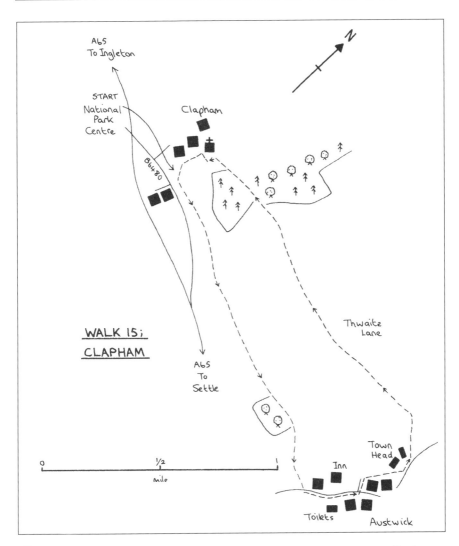

A65
To Ingleton

START
National
Park
Centre

Clapham

B6480

WALK 15;
CLAPHAM

A65
To
Settle

Thwaite
Lane

0   ½   1
mile

Town
Head

Inn

Toilets   Austwick

☺ There are blackberries along here. Some people call these
brambles which is an old word which used to be used by Vikings
who came to live in the Dales over a thousand years ago. The path
over the fields here is going to take us to Thwaite Lane. Thwaite is
another Norse word – meaning clearing.

*Scandinavian colonists founded many villages in the north of England
during the Dark Ages. The place names they gave places survive to this*

day. Austwick is one. 'Wick' denotes a settlement of Norwegian origin.
York itself is a diminutive of Jorvik (vik = wick).

**Cross the ladder stile and cross the field by walking up to the crest
with the dry**

**First until you reach the crest of this second field. Bear right to
bisect a line between the wall corner to your left and a large
limestone boulder to your right. This leads you to a further ladder
stile to cross onto Thwaite Lane. Head left.**

The rock outcrop to your right is Robin Proctor's Scar which fringes the
hill of Norber.

☺ That hill on the right is limestone. It is called Norber. When the
limestone is attacked by the weather, including frost, blocks of it
fall off. These form the piles of loose rock called screes which you
can see at the foot of the scar.

**Keep following Thwaite Lane until there is a T-junction of tracks at
the edge of a plantation.**

Q: What do most of the trees in the plantation here have in
common?

A: They are coniferous.

☺ Coniferous trees are mostly evergreen, but not all of them are. The
word coniferous just means that they have cones in them. Let's
see if we find any.

**Head left along the track that leads downhill. The track takes you
through two tunnels and into Clapham next to the church.**

The tunnels are part of the landscaping work that was done on the
grounds of Ingleborough Hall where Clapham Beck was dammed to create
a lake.

Turn right to walk past the church.

To the left here you will see an adventure playground.

On the way down to the village notice a white bridge stone – WR, West
Riding.

☺ In the past Yorkshire was divided up into three parts called ridings
and each was made its own county. Clapham was in the West
Riding. The other two were the North Riding, which included

Signpost in Clapham with "W.R." for West Riding *(Graham Beech)*

Swaledale, and the East Riding. This system was changed in the 1970s but many Yorkshire people still like to remember the old ridings and so markers like this have been left.

Wander down the village to return to the National Park Centre.

Bridges allow you to stroll along either bank of Clapham Beck.

Other Places of Interest in the Area:

Clapham and Ingleborough Cave

The chocolate-box village of Clapham (Walk 15) lies either side of Clapham Beck 7 miles north-west of Settle, off the A65. Ingleborough Cave (Tel: 014685 242) is nearby. Guided tours of the cave include probably the longest stalactite in Britain (1.5 metres). There are plentiful cafés and bar meal opportunities in Clapham.

Ingleborough Cave

See Walk 15.

Ingleton Waterfalls

See Walk 8.

White Scar Cavern

See Walk 8.

16. Conistone

Conistone is a chocolate box village with idyllic village green and Maypole. It is set in Wharfedale, opposite the impressive rock formation of Kilnsey Crag. The walk begins and ends at Conistone and circles, via the foot of Kilnsey Crag, Kilnsey Park Centre where there are ducks and fish for children to feed, a museum and aquarium, adventure playground and coffee shop/restaurant.

Starting point: Conistone Bridge (SD 979675)

Distance: Route A 2½ miles; Route B 1½ miles

Terrain: Across flat meadowland to Kilnsey, following a slightly uphill lane to the highest point on the walk. The descent over pasture land is only moderately downhill and terminates in easily walked lanes.

Map: OS Explorer OL2 Yorkshire Dales: Southern and Western Areas.

Toilets: Kilnsey Park Centre and Tennant Arms, Kilnsey

Refreshments: Kilnsey and Kilnsey Park

Pushchairs: The circular route would not be suitable although sections of it, in and around Conistone and Kilnsey, which follow lanes, would be easily manageable.

☺ You should pass most of these things on your walk. See how many you can spot.

☐ black and white cattle
☐ dry stone walls
☐ a horse rider
☐ a stone bridge
☐ a rock climber
☐ wildflowers, perhaps a bluebell

☐ a mountain bike

☐ an overhanging cliff

☐ a lake

☐ a quarry

☐ a pheasant

☐ a broadcasting mast

Walking away from Coniston village, cross Conistone Bridge over the River Wharfe.

☺ This river is called the River Wharfe and the whole valley is called Wharfedale. From the bridge we can see up and down Wharfedale. Which way is the river flowing?

☺ The rock cliff over there **(INDICATE AHEAD AND RIGHT)** is Kilnsey Crag. We will be walking up to it.

As soon as you have crossed the bridge, turn right through a narrow metal gate and down a few steps. Follow the path across

Kilnsey Crag *(Graham Beech)*

the grassy flood plain, waymarked to Scar Lathe. This path leads onto a rough track which follows the dry stone wall on your left.

☺ This wall (INDICATE LEFT) is a dry stone wall.

Q: Why do you think that is?

A: It has been built without any mortar to hold the stones to-gether. The wall builder has to carefully choose stones so that they will fit and stay in the wall.

Where there is a right-angled corner in the wall, bear left and walk diagonally towards the next corner where there is a single small tree.

Q: Do you know what type of tree this is?

A: It is a sycamore tree. You can tell this by the shape of the leaf. In autumn seeds fall in "spinners" which you can spin through the air like miniature frisbees.

From the tree, follow the wall until you reach two wooden gates. Turn right and walk on, ignoring a single wooden gate on the left which is opposite the Tennant Arms. Follow the farm track and line of telegraph poles.

☺ Over there (INDICATE RIGHT, TO THE OPPOSITE SIDE OF THE DALE) you can see outcrops of a type of rock that is very common in this part of the Yorkshire Dales – limestone. Limestone is special because water can attack it so that it dissolves. Underground caves and caverns have been made in this way.

Reaching the next right-angled corner of the wall, turn left and head towards the barn at Scar Lathe. Walk around the right-hand side of the building to wooden gates. Pass through these to the roadside.

☺ The cliff on the other side of the road is Kilnsey Crag. See how it overhangs. Some people go rock climbing on the crag.

The road can be busy, especially in summer.

Cross the road carefully and turn left along its edge. Keep going until you reach the Tennant Arms hotel.

The Tennant Arms is an inn with picnic tables and garden. The flag-stone floored bar serves meals and real ales.

Route A: Immediately beyond the Tennant Arms, turn right along the single track road marked as unsuitable for motor vehicles. Continue straight ahead when a road joins you from the left.

Route B: To short-cut the walk, continue along the road until you turn left down the lane to Conistone Bridge, signposted in the direction of St Mary's Church and Conistone Village.

Route B does have the advantage of passing the entrance to Kilnsey Park Centre.

☺ This is Kilnsey. It is a very small place and is called a hamlet because it does not have a church. Conistone is a little larger and does have a church.

Q: What sort of a settlement is Conistone?
A: A village.

Keep walking along the lane, uphill.

Look out for an old building on the right which has mullioned windows.

☺ The windows here are small and set directly in the thick stone walls. This is a very old way of building and these are called mullioned windows.

Continue to follow the lane as it swings left and upward out of Kilnsey and over a cattle grid.

☺ This is a cattle grid.

Q: What do you think it is for?
A: Animals will not cross the bars of the grid because of the gaps. So any which are grazing on the open land above the hamlet will not wander into Kilnsey. At the same time, traffic can pass freely along the road without having to stop to open and shut a gate.

☺ Along here **(INDICATE RIGHT)** are loose rocks called scree. This is made from limestone which has been broken off the main

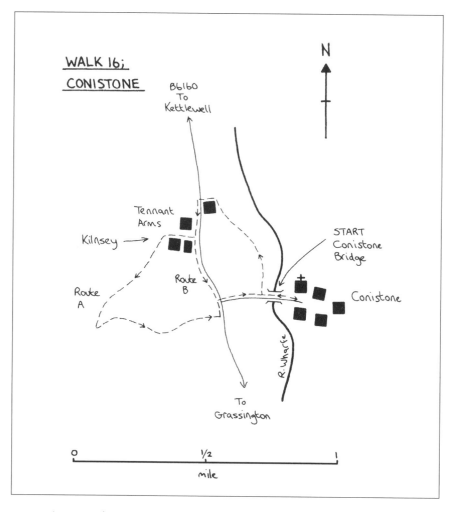

outcrops above by the action of frost. Water soaks into gaps, or joints, in the limestone and expands when it freezes at night. After many, many times, the limestone breaks off and falls down to make these screes.

Keep walking along the lane until there is a fork. The surfaced road heads right and there is a rougher track to the left. There is a waymark post.

☺ Run ahead to the waymark post and find out what it says.

A: Malham, 5 miles.

Head left along the bridleway in the direction of Malham.

☺ These **(INDICATE RIGHT)** are recently planted young trees called saplings.

Q: Why are they fenced off?
A: To protect them from grazing animals.

Pass through the metal gate you reach across your way.

☺ The rock on the right here is limestone. Their are clear cracks called joints in this rock which break it up into blocks. Some blocks of the limestone have been broken away by the frost and have fallen down towards the track here.

It is not very far to your turn off the bridleway. Watch the line of the dry stone wall on your left. As the bridleway begins to rise rightwards there is a right-angled corner into a small triangular inset. In the corner is a small wooden gate through which you pass to emerge atop a stone stile. Descend into the pasture beyond.

This stone stile is steep to descend and younger children would be well advised to wait of accompanying adults before passing through the wooden gate.

Follow the path ahead towards some ruins.

☺ The corner we have just turned was very sudden. This is because it is where travellers in the past would have taken a right fork after coming over the moors from Malham to make their way down to Conistone village.

Cross the tiny stone bridge beside the ruin. Walk on to the track which sweeps down from the right. Join it and head left, down the hill. Pass through the seven bar gate you come to and carry on beyond the point where a further track joins from the left to pass through a wooden gate that leads you on between a fence on your right and barn to the left.

☺ There is Kilnsey Crag again **(INDICATE LEFT)**. You can see its overhanging shape very clearly from here.

Continue along the farm lane until it meets the road. Turn left along the road until you can turn right in the direction of St Mary's church and Conistone.

Routes A and B have now converged. Walk on across Conistone Bridge and into the village.

In the centre of the first open space you encounter is a tall Maypole – Maypole Cottage is just by.

☺ This tall pole is the village Maypole. There is a tradition that people, especially children, dance around these poles with ribbons – in May, of course.

Other Places of Interest in the Area

Upper Nidderdale

Nidderdale to the north of Pateley Bridge is Upper Nidderdale. As well as the two walks described in this book (11 and 14), attractions include Gouthwaite Reservoir and How Stean Gorge. The latter is described as Yorkshire's "Little Switzerland" and is a narrow limestone gorge along which it is possible to walk. There is a café and children's play area adjacent to the car park. (Tel 01423 75666).

Kilnsey Park and Trout Farm, Conistone

Kilnsey Park is in Wharfdale just to the west of Conistone Village and is a leisure park offering a variety of attractions including children's adventure playground and fun fishing as well as the Trout Farm itself and the Dales Life Centre. There is a café and shop. The park is open every day (Tel 01756 752150) and is on the B6160 road. Website: www.kilnseypark.co.uk.

Kilnsey Trekking and Riding Centre, Conistone

In Conistone village itself is the Kilnsey Pony Trekking Centre. Safe riding can be arranged here for beginners as well as the more experienced. Telephone in advance for details (01756 752861/753369).

Grassington

See next walk.

17. *Grassington*

Grassington is the capital of Upper Wharfedale. There is much of historic interest including the recently restored folds – alleyways of workers' cottages, dating from the lead mining days of the 17th-19th centuries, which are a particular feature of the town. The Upper Wharfedale Museum is on the cobbled market place. It is a tourist honeypot so there is a wealth of cafés and pubs offering bar meals.

The walk itself includes a long avenue of horse chestnut trees along the Wharfe which make it particularly attractive in autumn – not least for the conker collector!

The turning point of this relatively long walk is Hebden which offers a range of refreshment facilities, as well as toilets.

Starting point: The National Park Centre car park (SE 002637), off the road into the village from Pateley Bridge

Distance: Route A, 5¼ miles; Route B, 1¾ miles.

Terrain: The route begins with an easy path down to the river and onto a lane leading to stepping stones. Then there is a long grassy riverside stretch, succeeded by a metalled lane up to Hebden. The walk then crosses pasture fields from Hebden before returning to Grassington via an unsurfaced lane.

Map: OS Explorer OL2 Yorkshire Dales: Southern and Western Areas.

Public Toilets: Grassington (including nappy change facilities at the National Park Centre) and Hebden

Refreshments: Grassington and Hebden

Pushchairs: Around Grassington village itself and along the lane at the end of the walk. The early stretch from Grassington car park down to Linton Falls and beyond as far as the church is also viable.

☺ You should pass most of these things on your walk. See how many you can spot.

☐ a waterfall

☐ stepping stones

☐ a suspension bridge

☐ brown cattle

☐ a black sheep

☐ an oak tree

☐ an angler

☐ a weir

☐ a duck

☐ a bath used for plants

☐ a rabbit burrow

☐ a goose

The Square, Grassington *(Graham Beech)*

Begin the walk in the car park by heading towards its frontage onto the main road. Turn right along the inside of the front wall and pass through a wooden kissing gate to a waymark sign. Turn right along Sedber Lane.

Q: Which waterfall are we walking towards?
A: Linton Falls

At the end of the cul-de-sac continue straight along the path with dry stone walls on either side of you. Walk right down to the footbridge at Linton Falls. Cross it and walk onto the viewing area to the left.

> A range of rock features formed by river erosion at the falls are evident including plunge pools, pot-holes and a minor but discernible gorge downstream.

☺ If you look at the rocks here you can see holes in them called pot-holes. The waterfall has made these by swirling stones around to drill the pot-holes. The bigger pools where the water spills over are called plunge pools.

> Indicate right, downstream.

☺ Over there are low rocky cliffs on either side of the river. The waterfall used to be down there, but it has worn away the rock so much that it has moved back here.

Route A: From the end of the footbridge follow the path to the right behind some stone-built houses. Coming to a T-junction head left.

> To the right here is a small bridge where there are often ducks.

☺ Go along there as far as the little bridge. Are there any ducks there today?

Route B: To avoid the later stepping stones, turn round and cross the footbridge again. Take the riverside path on the right and follow it until you reach a gate across which the stepping stones are visible and you rejoin Route A.

On route A your path will bring you up to a minor road. Turn left along this and continue past a row of cottages on your left.

There are some public toilets at the end of the row. Beyond, a lone house stands to the right of a distinct river meander.

☺ Look at the river. On this side the bank is really steep – a river cliff. on the other side it is much gentler and there is a beach of stones. This is because the water over there on the inside of the bend is much slower than on this side. So, the river wears away on the outside, and leaves stones behind on the inside.

At the end of the lane, pass through metal gates into the churchyard.

The Church of St Michael and All Angels is medieval, at least fourteenth century, and probably stands on the site of an older pagan shrine.

☺ This church is very old. Parts of it were built in the fourteenth century.

Q: How long ago is that?

A: 600 years

Walk just a few paces along the paved path until a waymarked, unsurfaced footpath leads you along the right-hand fork. Follow this along the edge of the graveyard until you emerge at a gap in the dry stone wall. Pass through and walk across the pasture to cross the stepping stones.

☺ As we go across the stepping stones try and count how many there are, but be careful not to fall in!

There are 53 main stepping stones.

Scramble up the bank opposite.

Note, to the left, two gates and a waymark post together. Here routes A and B converge.

Escape route: Walk up to and through the gates. Bear left along the river back to Linton Falls.

To continue on Route A, follow the flat, broad grass track across

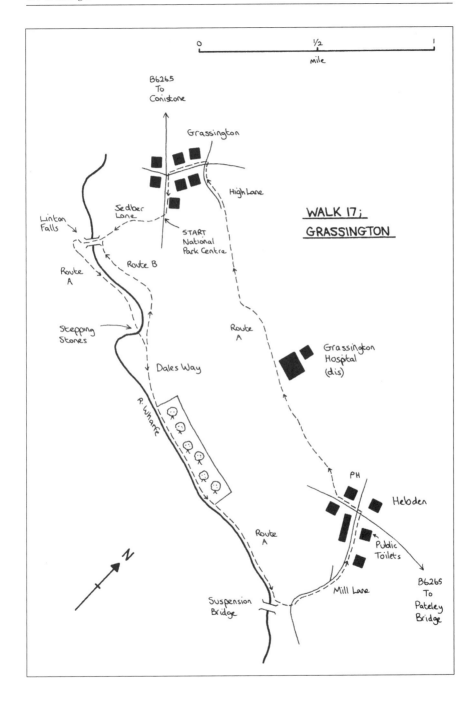

WALK 17;
GRASSINGTON

the middle of the pasture towards riverside trees in the distance, via a footbridge and a kissing gate.

Q: What kind of trees are most of these?

A: Horse chestnut

This stretch of the walk follows a section of the long distance Dales Way path which winds its way throughout the national park.

Follow the riverside path until you reach the suspension footbridge at Hebden. Walk right up to it.

The suspension bridge at Hebden is Victorian – the green lattice ironwork is a typical period feature. Children are likely to want to go on the bridge, but the route itself does not cross it.

☺ Look for a plaque and find out who built this bridge and how old it is.

The bridge was built by local blacksmith William Bell in 1885.

Turn left to walk up the path away from the bridge. Pass through the gate on the left at the end. Once in the pasture, bear right and walk up to the next gate which takes you onto the metalled Mill Lane.

Q: This lane is called Mill Lane. Why do you think that might be?

A: It leads down from Hebden village to the river where the water would have powered the mill.

Walk up the lane to your left. This takes you into Hebden village. Stick to this main lane all the way to the main road.

In Hebden the local shop and post office sells snacks, drinks and ice cream. There are public toilets and a children's playground. The Clarendon pub serves bar snacks.

Turn left at the cross-roads, signposted Grassington. Continue as far as the bus and lorry depot on the right. Immediately beyond, take the second of two waymarked footpaths on the right, in the direction of Grassington.

Q: What does this post tell us about the way to Grassington?

A: It is via High Lane.

Escape route: Instead of turning along the footpath, walk along the road all the way into Grassington.

The path brings you to a stone stile which you cross before following it as it wends its way leftwards. Keep the field boundary on your right until you reach another stone stile to cross.

☺ This stile is waymarked by a yellow painted spot. This tells us we are going the right way – that this is a footpath everyone can use.

Cross the next pasture to a small wood gate. Coming to a farm track, walk a little along it, to your right, until you reach the dry stone wall. Keep this on your right and make for the stile that takes you into the woods.

Grassington Park is the grounds of the former Grassington Hospital. It is now protected as a site of special scientific interest.

☺ This area is one where the plants are very unusual. There are wild herbs here that no longer grow elsewhere in the area. So, it is protected and is called a Site of Special Scientific Interest.

Emerging from the woods, walk on over the open area to a crossing of several tarmac paths.

The buildings on your right are the now disused Grassington Hospital.

Keep going until you cross the main drive and follow the path through a further short stretch of trees to a stone stile. Cross it, and its successor, to come to a field with a Dales barn on your right.

☺ These isolated stone barns are typical of the Yorkshire Dales. They are called Dales Barns. Farmers can store animal feed and equipment in them, and animals can use them for shelter up on the daleside, well away from the main farmyard.

Carry on until you cross a farm lane and then follow the track ahead until it sweeps temptingly left. Avoid the temptation! Follow the dry stone wall on your right as far as the corner. Then bear left across the field to cross the stile in the top corner.

☺ This is the lane that the waymark sign in Hebden mentioned.

Q: Can you remember what it is called?

A: High Lane

Follow High Lane to Grassington. Turn right onto the first metalled
road and then left down the main street. Head left along the road at
the end to return to the National Park Centre.

Other Places of Interest in the Area

Parcevall Hall Gardens, Appletreewick

The gardens here include orchards, splashing streams and woodland walks. There is a picnic area. They are open daily from Easter to
October (Tel 01756 720311). Appletreewick is about 5 miles
south-east of Grassington, off the B6160 towards Ilkley. Website:
www.parcevallhallgardens.co.uk.

Kilnsey Park and Trout Farm

See Walk 16.

Bolton Abbey

See Walk 9.

18. Settle

Settle is a bustling market town just to the south-west of the national park boundary. The market square with the Shambles arcade and quaint back streets and yards make it an especially attractive place to wander. There is a wealth of cafés and eateries, including the famous Ye Olde Naked Man.

The Museum of North Craven Life and the Watershed Mill Craft Centre on Langcliffe Road which features children's art activity are possible points of interest for children in Settle itself. The Yorkshire Dales Falconry and Conservation Centre near Giggleswick (follow the signs from Settle) is nearby.

The walk takes you alongside the River Ribble, following part of the Ribble Way, and then over fields to the very pretty village of Langcliffe before returning high up on the side of the dale to Settle. The going underfoot is stony at times and stout footwear is essential for comfort and safety.

Starting point: Whitefriars car park (SD 818637). This signposted car and coach park is at the northern end of the main street (the far end if you drive in from the A65).

Distance: 3¼ miles

Terrain: Once the walk reaches the riverside it proceeds along unsurfaced paths mixed with surfaced lanes as far as Langcliffe. The walk then climbs and crosses pastureland before descending a very stony lane back into Settle.

Map: OS Explorer OL2 Yorkshire Dales: Southern and Western Areas.

Public Toilets: Settle

Refreshments: Settle

Pushchairs: Other than Settle itself, and around the pretty green village of Langcliffe, this walk is not suited to pushchairs

☺ You should pass most of these things on your walk. See how many you can spot.

☐ a viaduct

☐ a church spire

☐ a mill chimney

☐ an ash tree

☐ a horse

☐ a beech tree

☐ a river lock

☐ a sycamore tree

☐ a blackberry bush

☐ a green dome

☐ a sign to Malham

☐ a café with no clothes on!

Walk out of the front of the car park and turn left, away from the town centre, and walk under the viaduct and down to the bridges over the River Ribble.

☺ The river here is called the Ribble and Settle is in the lower part of Ribblesdale.

Horton-In-Ribblesdale is the starting point for another walk in this book (walk 12) and so is Ribblehead (8). If you have already done either of these you may want to point out the geographical connection.

Cross the white-railed footbridge.

Q: Now we are crossing out of Settle. Where are we coming into?

A: Giggleswick (there is a sign).

Cross the road carefully and take the footpath between the school grounds and the football pitch.

☺ This part of the walk is along the Ribble Way – a long distance footpath that people can use to walk right along Ribblesdale.

Continue over the next stile and along the grassy path beyond. Keep the wall, and then fence, on your left, crossing a stile on the

way, to another beyond which you bear left and walk diagonally to the left to cross the dry stone wall stile onto the metalled lane. Turn right along this.

☺ The waymarking along here tells us we are on the Ribble Way. There is a blue R above a blue W. The letters are wavy. This is all to make it look like the river surface.

Walk along the lane to the fork. If you want to explore the hamlet of Stackhouse bear left here and walk round the loop to rejoin the route on the other side of the settlement.

Otherwise, bear right and continue along the lane (waymarked Ribble Way) to pass the house of Ribblelands on the right.

This is where the road from Stackhouse comes back in on the left.

Turn right down the track signposted `Ribble Way, Locks'.

A notable limestone scar is visible on the right – Stainforth Scar. Point it out.

☺ Over to the left is a limestone cliff. These cliffs are called scars, and that one is Stainforth Scar.

At the end, cross the footbridge.

☺ The weirs and locks here are to control the water which is taken from the Ribble here to use in the mill we passed earlier.

Bear left of the houses and walk up the metalled lane to the road. Cross the road carefully and then walk over the wooden footbridge to your right.

☺ This is over the railway. The Settle to Carlisle railway is a famous route which crosses the huge Ribblehead Viaduct to the north of Horton in Ribblesdale.

The Ribblehead viaduct is featured by Walk 8.

As soon as you have crossed the railway, turn left down a waymarked lane and look for a waymarker on the right, before you reach the wooden gate.

Escape route: Carry on alongside the road and return to Settle.

Turn right through a single gate and walk along the left side of the pasture, over the crest, and pass through the next gate onto a lane. Turn right and walk into Langcliffe village.

☺ This village is Langcliffe.

Langcliffe is a lovely green Dales village. Seats around the green make it an inviting half-way picnic stop. There is children's play equipment here. There is a Post Office, but no village shop.

Leave Langcliffe by walking back up the green to pass the school on your left. Just in front of the dry stone wall which crosses the line of the road, bear right and uphill to a wooden gate. Pass through and continue uphill to the top corner of this pasture.

There are views here back over Langcliffe.

Turn right through the gate and follow the track which follows the dry stone wall on the right.

☺ Look over the wall here. We can see down the dale, as far as Settle itself.

After passing a small enclosure of trees, go through a single wooden gate.

☺ Look right here for a green-domed building. This is above the village of Giggleswick where there is a famous public school.

It was here that the late television personality Russell Harty used to teach.

Continue ahead until you cross a ladder stile and head right alongside the dry stone wall. Keep going and the way becomes effectively a green lane, with dry stone walls to either side. Pass through the farm gate you come to, and continue.

☺ We can see the viaduct (over to the right) where we parked. The railway over it is the Settle-Carlisle line we crossed over earlier, before we reached Langcliffe.

On the left is a waymark sign to Malham – some 5 miles away across the moors.

Carry straight on, downhill. Pass through a single wooden gate to the left of a ruin. Follow the stony lane ahead down into Settle.

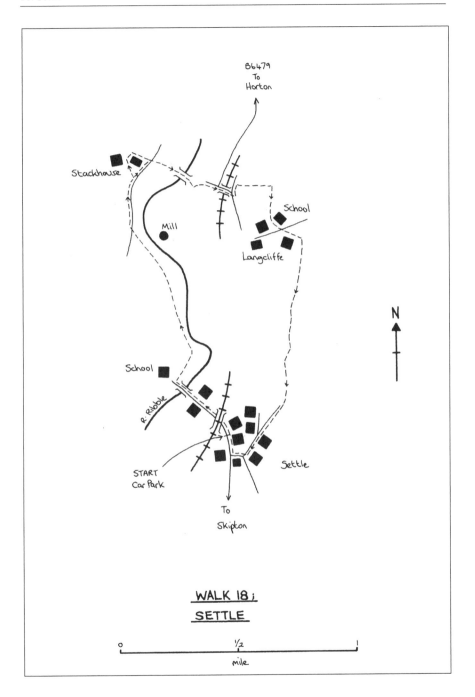

B6479
To
Horton

Stackhouse

Mill

School

Langcliffe

School

R. Ribble

START
Car Park

Settle

To
Skipton

N

WALK 18;
SETTLE

0   ½   1
mile

Settle station *(Graham Beech)*

Bear initially left and then keep going down to reach the main street. The Whitefriars car park will be to the right.

Other Places of Interest in the Area

Malham

The village of Malham (Walk 19) is a busy place because of the many visitors to nearby Malham Cove. There are numerous cafés and refreshment facilities, and the green, stone bridges and ducks in the beck make it a pleasant place to visit for itself.

Malham Cove is a crescent-shaped limestone scar a short walk from the village (see Walk 19). The cliff is 250 feet in height (76 metres). In the past it was a waterfall, but the rainwater now sinks into the limestone rock and only a small stream now emerges at the cove foot.

Ribblehead Viaduct

See Walk 8.

Clapham

See Walk 15.

19. *Malham*

Malham Cove is a crescent-shaped limestone scar. The cliff is 250 feet in height (76 metres). In the past it was a waterfall, but the rainwater now sinks into the limestone rock and only a small stream emerges at the cove foot.

Malham village is the start and finish point of the walk. This is a busy place because of the many visitors to the cove. There are numerous cafés and refreshment facilities. The green, stone bridges and ducks in the beck make it a pleasant place to spend time in after your walk.

The walk itself can be kept more or less on the level if you follow the shorter and much quicker Route B. To do the full Route A you need to be prepared for the over 300 steps up to the limestone pavement and for the crossing of this rocky wilderness. This is high and exposed moorland and you must be well shod and waterproofed. You also need clear visibility to appreciate the views as well as to see where you are.

Starting point: National Park Centre, Malham (SD 900637)

Distance: Route A: 2¾ miles; Route B: 2 miles

Terrain: From the village to Malham Cove the walk is over surfaced lanes and paths. Route B returns over gentle pasture. Route A climbs the steps up the side of the cove and traverses the limestone pavement at the summit before returning via higher pasture and the lane of Malham Rakes.

Map: OS Explorer OL2 Yorkshire Dales: Southern and Western Areas.

Public Toilets: Malham

Refreshments: Malham

Pushchairs: The stretch from the village to the cove and back is suitable

☺ You should pass most of these things on your walk. See how many you can spot.

☐ a stone bridge

☐ a duck

☐ a Pennine Way sign

☐ a horse chestnut tree

☐ a tent

☐ a limestone boulder

☐ a footbridge

☐ an ash tree

☐ the source of a stream

☐ a limestone cliff

☐ a clint

☐ brown cattle

Limestone pavement, Malham *(Graham Beech)*

Walk out of the national park centre car park and turn left to walk through the village, bearing left at the fork in the centre to follow the lane towards Malham Cove.

Pass Townhead Farm camp-site on your right, walk on a little further and then turn right towards the cove, signposted Pennine Way, through a kissing gate. Follow the path down to the cove itself.

☺ You can see the source of Malham Beck here, flowing out from beneath the foot of the cove.

From the cove face, begin to re-trace your steps.

Route A: Where the paths fork, just after the wood gate, branch right and walk up to the flight of steps which have been built to the side of the cove.

☺ These steps have been made like this because of all the wearing away of the slope caused by too many walkers coming here. Do you think it is a good idea?

This is issue has provoked different attitudes including the positive side of erosion limitation, neatening the appearance and using blending materials, as well as the negative of introducing an air of urbanism to a wild area and doubt as to whether the materials do blend successfully. What do your children think?

Route B: Walk back further along the valley to a bend in the beck where a footbridge crosses it to the left, to a waymarked gate. Follow the path through the gate and back to the village.

Route A: Ascend the steps.

The author counted 368 of these in total. How many do you make it?

☺ On the way up let's see if we can count the steps. Try to do it in stages. We could start with how many there are to the gate.

(15)

Near the top the stepped path turns sharply left in front of a rock face.

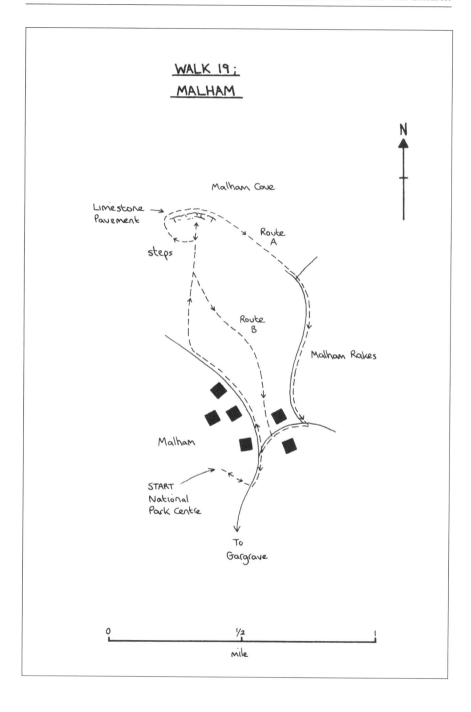

☺ This rock is limestone. You can see how it is jointed. These crevices are the joints and they give the limestone a structure of blocks. Rainwater can react with the limestone to make it dissolve and enlarge these joints. Frost can also penetrate and expand the joints. Blocks become loose because of this weathering and fall off. The screes of broken limestone we can see along the dale **(INDICATE)** have been made in this way.

The process of frost action involves water penetrating joints, freezing and expanding to exert pressure on the rock. Nightly repetitions over very many freeze-thaw cycles can eventually weaken the rock. It is likely that in modern Britain there is insufficient frost to make very much difference and that the screes are relics of colder climate following the retreat of the ice which began about 18 000 years ago.

Reaching the top of the path, cross the ladder stile you encounter and head first left and then right to the notice board and then head to the right to cross the limestone pavement which is at the top of the cove.

Care is needed here. The gaps (grykes) are often deep (up to 2m and more) and are easy to catch your foot in to trip, or twist an ankle.

☺ This bare rock is called a limestone pavement. It is made up of blocks of limestone called clints which are separated by enlarged joints (grykes). Be careful how you tread.

At the far side of the limestone pavement is a ladder stile to cross.

To the right is the cliff edge. Walk a little towards this to admire the view but keep well clear of the edge itself.

☺ We are now at the top of the cove. You can see down to where we walked before and back along the valley to Malham village where we began.

From the ladder stile bear slightly right to walk to the left of a low dry stone wall and fence until they meet a larger wall. Turn left and walk along with the wall on

Skirt a rocky depression, in which there are some ruins, to their left. As the path dips to the right and passes to the left of a dry stone walled mound, follow it to the ladder stile ahead.

Cross over to the metalled lane and turn right to follow this down into Malham village.

Indicate the village.

 You can see Malham village again from here. That is where we are heading.

Other Places of Interest in the Area

Malham Tarn

Malham Tarn is a lake which together with its immediate surroundings has been classified as a site of special scientific interest. The lake can be accessed on foot, along the Pennine Way, from the minor road which leads north from Malham village towards Arncliffe.

Gordale Scar

Gordale Scar is a spectacular limestone gorge 1¼ miles to the east of the walk described here. On the return walk to Malham, turn left where Gordale is signposted and follow the path to Gordale Scar, returning to Malham via Gordale Lane – this will add 2½ miles to your walk.

Settle

See Walk 18.

20. Bolton Abbey

A straightforward and pleasant walk along the banks of the River Wharfe, taking in the ruins of historic Bolton Priory on the way.

This is not to be confused with Bolton Castle in Wensleydale (walk 3).

Bolton Priory was first established by Augustinian monks in the twelfth century and was ruined during the sixteenth-century dissolution of the monasteries. Its magnificent setting makes a dramatic starting point for this walk along the Strid – as this stretch of the Wharfe is known.

Starting point: Bolton Abbey car park – the first you reach as you drive up from Bolton Bridge and the A59. (SE 071539)

Distance: 2½ miles

Terrain: Mostly grass paths and gentle, with a couple of slightly steeper sections along the way.

Map: OS Explorer OL2 Yorkshire Dales: Southern and Western Areas.

Public Toilets: Bolton Abbey

Refreshments: Bolton Abbey (car park and village) and Bolton Bridge

Pushchairs: From the car park to the priory and riverside and back is pushchairable as, in dry weather, is the stretch on the abbey side to Bolton Bridge and back.

☺ You should pass most of these things on your walk. See how many you can spot.

☐ ducks

☐ black and white cattle

☐ a seat made from a tree trunk

☐ an acorn (in Autumn)

☐ an ash tree

☐ a wind power generator

☐ a tree stump

☐ a river meander

☐ a stone bridge

☐ a tractor

☐ stepping stones

☐ a stately home

Bolton Abbey *(Norman Buckley)*

From the car park walk towards the information office and refreshment kiosk. Follow the waymark sign to the priory, right towards the village green.

Bolton Abbey village is an estate village.

🙂 This village is an estate village. It was built by the Duke of Devonshire, the landowner, to house the people who work for him on the estate.

Bear left alongside the triangular green and look for the entrance hole in the stone wall on the other side of the road.

Walk through the gate.

Pause to look at the board which shows an artist's recreation of the Bolton Abbey of the early sixteenth century, as viewed from this vantage point.

🙂 Look at this drawing of what the abbey used to be like. Try and match up what the artist has drawn with the ruins you can see below us.

Descend the steps. Walk down to the priory ruins.

If you have a pushchair the steps are avoidable by following the signed disabled route from the entrance gate. Take time to explore the ruins themselves.

🙂 These ruins are just parts of the walls of the original abbey. Try to imagine roofs and windows – some of them stained glass, and all the walls fully built. There would have been monks around too, and people coming and going. There was the main church where the monks would have prayed, but also other ordinary buildings – like a bakery – to look after the needs of the monks.

🙂 The abbey was built between 600 and 700 years ago and has been a ruin for 400 years.

From the ruins, cross the footbridge over the Wharfe.

To the left of the footbridge stepping stones make a more adventurous alternative.

Turn left along the river bank for a short way until the path

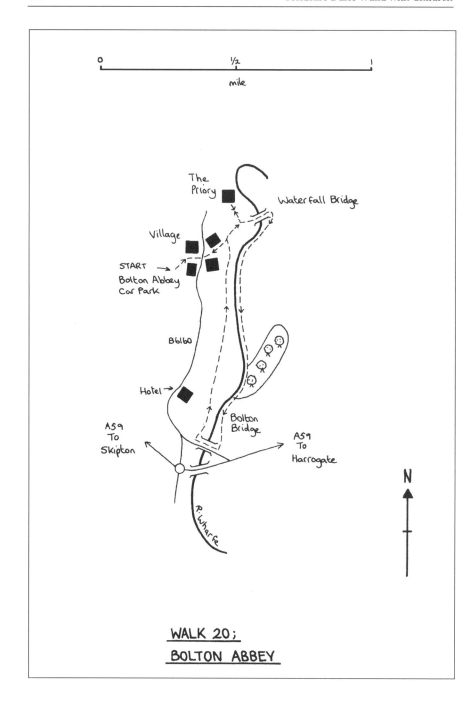

WALK 20;
BOLTON ABBEY

divides. Take the right fork up a short flight of steps and walk on, to the right, up to a seat.

☺ There are newly planted trees along here. One of the types of tree here will grow acorns in years to come.

Q: What type of tree is that?
A: Oak

☺ See if you can recognise an oak.

Turn right along the next path. It is waymarked.

Q: Where does the sign point to?
A: Storiths

☺ We are not actually going to Storiths. We are going to walk to walk alongside the River Wharfe to Bolton Bridge, so we will have to watch for another waymark sign soon.

Walk up the path to the skyline where there is another waymark post.

Q: Which way do we go now?
A: Straight on, because that is the way to Bolton Bridge.

Go straight on and cross the stile you reach. Carry on across a wooden footbridge to the next stile on your right. Cross this and continue. Soon you are walking along with a short avenue of trees to your left.

Here are many glimpses of the ruins to be had from along here.

☺ Keep looking through the trees to see the Abbey ruins below. Look out for ducks and geese too.

Keep hugging the fence-line on your right as it curves downwards to reach another stile to cross into a flat pasture. Cross the middle of this, making for the farm gate opposite.

From the gate, proceed to the next one and continue along the track as it rises to surmount a river cliff.

☺ This is called a river cliff **(INDICATE)**. Notice how it is on the outside of the river bend (or meander) where the current is stronger and can cut away at its base. This can cause it to collapse and move back, which may make it higher.

At the top, the track sweeps left into a pasture, but you need to bear right and down, with a dry stone wall to your left, to cross a stile. Follow the fence-line on your right as it brings you down to flood plain level and walk straight on towards the buildings of Red Lion Farm.

☺ This is Red Lion Farm and the bridge over to our right is Bolton Bridge. We will cross it soon and begin to walk back on the other side.

Find the waymark post beside a stile and cross this into a narrow path between the buildings. Emerging onto a metalled lane, turn right.

☺ This lane is the old road between Skipton and Blubberhouses which has been replaced by the wider, new one. So the bridge we are about to cross is the old bridge. You can see the new one over to its left.

Across Bolton Bridge, turn right through a small metal gate onto the waymarked footpath across the meadow.

Q: How far does the sign say it is back to Bolton Priory?
A: 3/4 mile.

  A seat by the river here may be a good picnic stop. To reach the café or hotel, which serves bar food, keep on the road and then come back to the metal gate to resume the walk after your break.

Follow the green path to a metal kissing gate. Beyond this the path diverges. Bear left, allowing the riverbank to drift off to the right, and head straight towards the now visible ruins.

  The riverside footpath rejoins later, so you can continue along it if you prefer.

When the paths have reconverged, continue along between the Wharfe and a wooded steep bank to your left. Cross the wider meadow ahead, keeping close to the river bank.

The river here is braided and, unless it is in flood, you should be able to see a gravelly island called an eyot.

☺ Look at the river here. You can see how the water splits and then joins again. This is called braiding – like if some-one has braids in their hair. The island is called an eyot. If the river is full, after heavy rain for instance, this island's gravel may be washed away for a time.

Cross the wooden footbridge you reach and then a stile to rejoin the path which brought you down to the priory at the beginning of the walk. Follow this back up to the village and car park.

Other Places of Interest in the Area

Barden Tower

Barden Tower is a historic hunting lodge west of Bolton Abbey – about 3 miles from the village, along the B6160 towards Grassington. It lies at the North end of the Duke of Devonshire's estate and has an adjacent tea room. Enquires: 01756 718009.

Embsay and Bolton Abbey Steam Railway

See Walk 21. There is a Bolton Abbey station on the Embsay and Bolton Abbey Steam Railway beside the A59 to Skipton. A footpath leads to it from Bolton Abbey; it ia a half-mile walk.

Skipton Castle

Skipton Castle (Tel 01756 792442) is one of the most complete medieval castles in the country. This means it still has a roof for wet days! Information tour sheets are provided and children receive a castle explorer's badge. The castle is in central Skipton and is open every day except Christmas Day, though not until 2pm on Sundays.

Skipton itself is a busy town – the gateway to the Dales – and provides a full range of shops and refreshments opportunities. Website: www.skiptoncastle.co.uk.

21. Embsay

Embsay is a former textiles village, two miles north of the town of Skipton – "gateway to the Dales". Embsay is particularly well known for its steam railway which may be a major plus of this walk for many children. The Embsay steam railway runs occasional special events including Thomas the Tank Engine days on some bank holidays. For details of these and the regular timetable, contact **01756 794727.** Website:www.embsayboltonabbeyrailway.org.uk

Embsay Crag is part of the Barden Moor open access area with views over Embsay Moor Reservoir at its foot, and its sailing club. Grouse nest here, as does the golden plover – in the shelter afforded by the heather. The vegetation around Embsay Crag is often as high as a small child. While the more adventurous will see this section of the walk as something of a jungle exploration you may need to be more cautious when choosing this walk for very young or sensitive children in high and late summer especially.

Starting point: Embsay car park (SE 008538)

Distance: 3½ miles (Routes A & B)

Terrain: The early part of the route is over pastures with frequent stone stiles. The going is relatively easy along the lane to the Embsay Crag open-access area but the latter is densely vegetated with heather and bracken and becomes quite steep on the approaches to the crag. The descent over fields is straightforward.

Map: OS Explorer OL2 Yorkshire Dales: Southern and Western Areas.

Toilets and Refreshments: Embsay Village

Pushchairs: If you by-pass the first section of the route by sticking to the metalled road, you can pushchair as far as the reservoir and back. To do this leave the car park by the front entrance and head right, across the front of the Elm Tree pub. Then bear right to follow the lane towards Embsay Moor Reservoir.

🙂 You should pass most of these things on your walk. See how many you can spot.

- ☐ a lake
- ☐ a sail
- ☐ a quarry
- ☐ a steam engine
- ☐ an old mill chimney
- ☐ black and white cattle
- ☐ a henhouse
- ☐ a goose
- ☐ a wind generator
- ☐ an ash tree
- ☐ brown cattle
- ☐ a lych gate

Begin the walk at the free public car park in the centre of Embsay village, adjacent to the Elm Tree inn. Leave the car park through the gate at the back and walk diagonally left.

Embsay Crag is immediately visible over to the right. The crag is 1217 feet (371 metres) above sea-level and the route may take you to its summit depending on what you choose to do when you arrive at its open access area.

🙂 The hill over there is called Embsay Crag. We are going to walk over to it today and pass a reservoir with sailing boats on the way.

Reach the stone steps in the far corner and climb them. Walk across the paddock you enter, bearing slightly right, to a footpath waymark post next to a corner of the school field. follow the path along the back of the school field and behind the farm beyond.

This first section of the walk is a little intricate across a number of small pastures. Children may like to go ahead to find the next way marker each time.

Cross the stone steps ahead and cross the farm lane and the

waymarked wooden stile beyond. Then turn left to walk around the field edge to cross the next stone stile, beside a waymark post.

Keep the house on your left as you bear right a little to a bush and then follow a short section of dry stone wall to some steps to climb over the next stone wall.

Beyond this make for a seven-bar gate.

Q How is this gate waymarked for us?
A By the yellow painted spot.

Cross the stile to its left. Walk straight ahead. Walk under a large solitary tree's boughs.

Q: What sort of tree is this?
A: Sycamore.

The wooden fence beside you becomes one of wood and wire. Near the end bear left through a roughly vegetated patch to descend to a waymarked stone stile across which you join a metalled lane.

Turn right along the lane.

   Escape route: Turn left and follow the lane back to Embsay

Walk down to the dip.

   There is a controlled water source here.

☺ Embsay Moor Reservoir itself has been managed since the last century, to provide water for people who live in the city of Bradford. You can also see one of the old mill chimneys from here.

Other industry in the Embsay area has long included quarrying. Looking right, in the direction of Embsay Crag, a quarry can be seen from here. It is its industrial heritage that accounts for the relatively large size of Embsay village, though clearly today many of the villagers are employed in Skipton and other towns.

Coming to a right-angled bend in the lane, there is a choice of ways. Head straight on past the sign for intake farm. Carry on to a T-junction and turn left along the bridleway in the direction of Embsay Crag.

Keep going along the stony lane and on past Craven Sailing Club. Keep going straight ahead until the lane leads to a gateway. Pass through this and cross the stile to your right into the open access area.

Barden Moor open access area is so-called because you are able to explore it without sticking simply to designated rights of way. It is nevertheless sensible to stay close to the paths and to keep young children within sight since the area is densely vegetated. There is also an old quarry within the area.

The rock hereabouts is gritstone rather than limestone. Soils are acidic as a result and so favour the heather and bracken vegetation which grows here in such profusion. Red grouse nest here among the heather which is burnt off every few years, a patch at a time, to keep it short and young.

At the information board, turn right to cross the stream and proceed to a waymark sign post. Follow the blue marker posts of the bridlepath and cross a footbridge close to the wall on your right.

From here on options open up for you.

Route A: **Continue to follow the blue waymarker posts and they will lead you up and over Embsay Crag.**

Views over the reservoir from here are splendid especially on a fine day when there are boats out.

Route B: **Alternatively you can follow the wallside footpath, though you may find the wall cuts off the view over the reservoir.**

Again, since this is an open access area you can wander more freely keeping the crag to your left and the reservoir to your right until the bracken ends when you have passed the crag by. However you need to be aware that there is an old quarry working here which children should not be tempted by.

When you clear the bracken, no matter which route you have taken, the ways converge and you need to look out for a waymark post by the wall pointing to Eastby via a small gate through the wall.

☺ Look over to the other side of the dale. You can see quite a big quarry and over to the left some tall propeller-like machines. These are wind-generators to convert wind energy into electricity.

Embsay Moor reservoir from the top of Embsay Crag *(Rebecca Terry)*

Some people like them because they do not make smoke to pollute the air.

Q: Local people are not always very keen. Can you think why not?

A: They can be noisy and some people think they spoil the view.

Go through the gate into the pasture and walk straight downhill. Follow the bridleway through a gate at the bottom of the field and enter a green lane.

Just before you enter the green lane, point out the spring on your left.

Continue to follow the track ahead until it approaches some farm buildings. Pass through the metal gate and walk on to pass the farmyard on your left. Keeping straight on, descend along the farm drive until it takes a marked leftward swing.

At this point there is a legal diversion, dating from 1977, of the footpath. Landowners can apply for this to be done if there is good reason, and an equally good or better alternative for walkers exists.

Follow the lane down to the minor road.

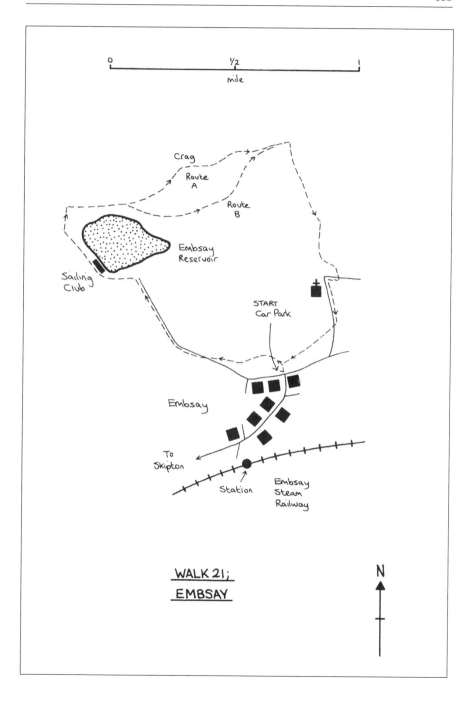

WALK 21;
EMBSAY

N

Indicate the cattle grid.

Q: What are these metal bars for?
A: They are to keep animals from wandering from the open graz-
    ing land behind us onto the road where there may be traffic.

**Turn right and walk alongside the minor road, rounding the sharp
left-hand bend. Pass the church of St Mary the Virgin on your right.
Immediately beyond the gate is a driveway and adjacent to this a
public footpath sign in the corner of the field.**

**Pass through the gate and into the field. Head diagonally towards
the far corner to cross the first of two succeeding pairs of stone
steps to emerge behind the car park start point.**

Other Places of Interest in the Area

Embsay and Bolton Abbey Steam Railway

Real steam trains ply the short stretch of track either side of Embsay
Station itself – 2½ miles to Holywell Halt. There are picnic areas at
both stations. Thomas the Tank Engine weekends are held on some
bank holidays. A return trip takes about 40 minutes. For timetable
and other information, telephone 01756 710614. Embsay is 2 miles
from Skipton and is signposted off the A59. Website:
www.embsayboltonabbeyrailway.org.uk

Bolton Abbey

There is a Bolton Abbey station on the Embsay and Bolton Abbey
Steam Railway beside the A59 to Skipton. A footpath leads to it from
Bolton Abbey; it ia a half-mile walk.

Skipton Castle

See Walk 20.

Parcevall Hall Gardens

See Walk 17.

More walks from Sigma:

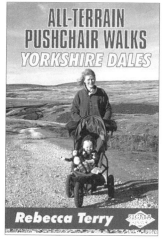

ALL-TERRAIN PUSHCHAIR WALKS: YORKSHIRE DALES

Rebecca Terry

30 pushchair walks in the countryside around the famous dales, including Nidderdale, and near to the major towns of Richmond, Harrogate, Skipton, Settle and Sedbergh. Riverside routes, moorland rambles and strolls around country estates, castles and abbeys. £7.95

YORKSHIRE DALES WALKING – ON THE LEVEL

Norman Buckley

All the pleasures of the dales without the climbs. This excellent guidebook leads you between the highest parts of this wonderfully scenic area for the very best views. "... a great buy."– *Ilkley Gazette* £6.95

NORTHUMBRIA WALKS WITH CHILDREN

Stephen Rickerby

By the same author as this book: 20 walks, suitable for families, covering the North East from the Tees to the Tweed. 'This is a splendid collection that will excite and stimulate youngsters.' – *Sunderland Echo* £6.95

All of our books are all available through booksellers. For a free catalogue, please contact: **SIGMA LEISURE, 5 ALTON ROAD, WILMSLOW, CHESHIRE SK9 5DY**
Tel/Fax: 01625-531035
E-mail: info@sigmapress.co.uk   Web site: www.sigmapress.co.uk